Tracy,
Continue to
dream.

A Black Woman's
Guide to Networking

Warmly,
Juliette Mayers

ISBN-10: 1456567780
ISBN-13: 9781456567781
LCCN: 2011917074
CreateSpace North Charleston, SC

A Black Woman's Guide to Networking

Advance Your Career.
Grow Your Business!

Juliette C. Mayers

Dedication

In memory of my loving mother, Evelyn C. Clarke

.

Contents

Praise for
A Black Woman's Guide to Networking

"This book is a powerful resource that will give readers effective networking strategies to succeed and achieve career and business goals."

> **Sheila A. Robinson**
> **Publisher of *Career Network* and *Diversity Woman* magazines**

"Juliette Mayers is an outstanding leader who has written a must-read book for those looking to accelerate their careers and business effectiveness."

> **Paul Guzzi**
> **President and CEO**
> **Greater Boston Chamber of Commerce**

"Juliette's book is an indispensible tool for women who really want to expand their base and use practical tips for effective networking. Professional development is a critical building block to achieve business success, and this book is a cornerstone."

> **Darnell L. Williams**
> **President and CEO**
> **Urban League of Eastern Massachusetts**

"Let the way you live your life speak for you. Live in the present, and reexamine yourself on all levels. Employ your powers and constantly remember a life without challenges is not worth living."

 Sheila Johnson
 Co-Founder, BET
 CEO and Founder, Salamander Hospitality LLC

"This is an important how-to book, and Juliette Mayers is the perfect seasoned executive to share her perspective about the value of networking to advance your career."

 Marian L. Heard
 President and CEO, Oxen Hill Partners
 Retired President and CEO
 The United Way of Massachusetts Bay and CEO of the United Ways of New England

Acknowledgments

I am thankful to God for the many blessings in my life. I have deep appreciation for the people who have supported me and continue to be the "wind beneath my wings."

Darryl, I am blessed, thrilled, and grateful to be married to you for the past twenty years. Thanks for your love, support and friendship. Without it, I would not have achieved this dream. Happy twentieth anniversary! I love you and look forward to many more years together as one.

Danielle and D'Anna, Nana would be so proud of you and the patience and support that you have given me throughout this process. You are two of the most beautiful young ladies on the planet—outside and inside. Your dad and I are so happy to have you in our lives.

This book is dedicated to my mom, who passed away at the age of fifty-seven—way too soon. Mom, I know that you are looking down from heaven and smiling proudly. Thanks for all of the sacrifices you made to make this present reality possible. To my dad Anthony Clarke a.k.a. Rudy, Rudolph, and Tony, thanks for believing in me.

Special acknowledgment goes to my sisters Maxcene Latin and Susan Archer. Thanks for your prayers, patience, and for always being there for me. Shout-outs to my ninety-two-year-old grandmother Doris Bascomb, and to my mother-in-law Elvoid Mayers, for her support, encouragement, and contribution to this book.

To my dear friend Martha R. A. Fields, I could not have done it without you. Thanks for believing in me and encouraging and coaching me through the process of writing this book. I appreciate you lovingly cracking the whip during the plateaus and am extremely grateful for the many hours spent reviewing each chapter. You are simply the best!

I'd like to acknowledge and thank some very special people who contributed to the book in the form of quotes, reviews, interviews, and expertise to a first-time author. I owe a huge debt of gratitude to each of the following people:

Stacy Blake-Beard, Ph.D., associate professor of management and faculty affiliate at the Center for Gender in Organizations, Simmons College

Josefina Bonilla, president, Color Media Group LLC, and publisher of *Color* magazine

Elizabeth G. Cook, former president, The Advertising Club of Greater Boston

Kathryn Dawson-Townsend, vice president, Member and Provider Service, Blue Cross Blue Shield, Massachusetts

Helen G. Drinan, president and CEO, Simmons College

Dr. Beverly Edgehill, president and CEO, The Partnership Inc.

Martha R. A. Fields, president and CEO, Fields Associates Inc.

Edie Fraser, senior consultant, Diversified Search

Cheryl Ginyard-Jones, managing principal, Energy and Utilities, Verizon Business

Jackie Glenn, chief diversity officer, EMC

Carolyn Golden-Hebsgaard, executive director, Lawyers Collaborative for Diversity Inc. and executive director of the Boston Law Firm Group

Tracey Gray-Walker, senior vice president and chief diversity officer, AXA Equitable

Paul Guzzi, president and CEO, Greater Boston Chamber of Commerce

Marian Heard, president and CEO, Oxen Hill Partners; retired president and CEO, the United Way of Massachusetts Bay; and the CEO of the United Ways of New England

Sheila Johnson, founder and CEO, Salamander Hospitality LLC

Elvoid Mayers, retired educator, chair of Social Studies Department, Rockland Public Schools

J. Keith Motley, Ph.D., chancellor, University of Massachusetts Boston

Colette A.M. Phillips, president and CEO, Colette Phillips Communications, founder of Get Konnected

Sheila Robinson, publisher, *Career Network* magazine and *Diversity Woman* magazine

Visael "Bobby" Rodriguez, chief diversity officer, Bay State Health

Dan Schawbel, managing partner, Millennial Branding LLC

Kathy Taylor, associate vice president, community development at Road Scholar

Patricia Washington, vice president and information security officer, Blue Cross Blue Shield Massachusetts

Linda Watters, vice president, government relations, John Hancock

Darnell L. Williams, president and CEO, The Urban League of Eastern Massachusetts

Introduction

Black women are poised to achieve career and business success. Throughout black America and globally, women have been the mothers, sisters, friends, business owners, and pillars in communities of faith. Within social circles many sisters display leadership skills and are adept at networking in churches, sororities, clubs, and organizations such as the Urban League, the NAACP, Jack & Jill of America, The Links Incorporated, and in their entrepreneurial ventures.

In corporate America and many structured organizations throughout the country, the picture is very different. There are very few blacks within leadership positions, and the news is worse for black women. In fact, as of 2010, there was only one black woman at the helm of a Fortune 500 company—Ursula Burns, CEO of Xerox.

The story is more optimistic outside corporate America and within the not-for-profit sector where a number of highly skilled black women are in powerful leadership roles. Some of the notables are:

- Susan Rice, U.S. Ambassador to the United Nations;
- Sheila Johnson, CEO of Salamander Hospitality
- Dr. Ruth Simmons, President, Brown University and first African American to head an Ivy League institution

- Judith Jamison, Artistic director, Alvin Ailey American Dance Theater
- Soledad O'Brien, Journalist, CNN
- Roslyn Brock, Chairman of the board, NAACP and
- Condoleezza Rice, former Secretary of State

There are several factors that contribute to a positive outlook for black women in the emerging worldview, and those who are skilled at networking will be best positioned to grow their businesses and advance their careers.

Three emerging trends will accelerate the pace of change for black women:

- Changing demographics and the increasing numbers of blacks in business and in organizations
- Increased visibility of business-savvy black women in media, education, politics, and entrepreneurial pursuits
- The rapid changes in technology and social media as a broadly accepted means of communicating, networking, and conducting business

The purpose of this book is to provide inspiration as well as practical tips and action-planning tools. While the primary target audience is professional black women, many of the themes are applicable to all professionals.

There are many books on networking. At its core, effective networking is about relationship building. It is common knowledge that the experiences and contributions of black women are nuanced by both race and gender. Many people know this to be true, but few acknowledge the undercurrent that is often present in the social and business interactions—the myths, fears, and perceived risks that often lead to lack of access, isolation, exclusion, and stagnation of careers and businesses. Unfortunately, there are no magic formulas for societal woes; however, there is an opportunity for black women to positively influence change and accelerate advancement.

Some of the networking principles in this book are universal. The diversity of perspectives rendered makes this book unique. As black women seek to break down barriers, it is critical that support systems extend beyond comfortable sister networks. The election of the first black president of the United States of America, Barack Obama, is an example of the kind of coalition building that is required to break down career and business barriers.

When I choose the title of this book, *A Black Woman's Guide to Networking: Advance Your Career. Grow Your Business!*, I received push back from some of my friends and more importantly from my twelve-year-old daughter, Danielle (now thirteen). "Mommy, you're not going to make many sales with that title. White people probably won't buy it." On the other hand, some of my white female friends said they would love to buy the book because those who are sincerely interested in building cross-cultural relationships would benefit. Both perspectives have merit. The reality is that there are those who question whether there is any difference between the professional experiences of black and white women. Aren't all women facing the same challenges?

For those of you who may want to gain deeper insights into the professional journey and why things are different for black women, I recommend that you read *Our Separate Ways: Black and White Women and the Struggle for Professional Identity* by Ella L. J. Edmondson Bell and Stella M. Nkomo. The book is based on eight years of research that was funded in part by the Rockefeller Foundation and the Ford Foundation. *Our Separate Ways* provides insights into the differences between black and white women's trials and triumphs on their way up the executive ladder. It is one of the few studies that examine the intersection of gender, race, and class for professional women. The book compares and contrasts the experiences of 120 black and white female managers in the American business arena.

Sadly, both black and white women remain largely underrepresented at the top of organizations. *Missing Pieces*, a 2010 Alliance for Board Diversity Census, documents the number of African American/black women on Fortune 100 boards of directors at 2.1 percent, which is virtually static compared to 2004 levels. At 4.2 percent, our black brothers are not much better off, and they've actually experienced a significant decline for the same period with 7.8 percent representation.

I share this information not to depress you. My hope is that you will take control of your environment and take the necessary actions to change these dismal statistics. It all begins with you—really!

I've completed a number of structured programs, including widely known leadership programs with GE Capital and the Executive Leadership Council's (ELC) Pipeline Leadership Program, a program designed to prepare high-potential black professionals for the C-Suite. Through my ELC experience I developed close relationships with a group of very special executive women—my "Pipeline Sisters." Some of them have contributed to this book. The ELC experience was the first time in my professional life that I could connect candidly with other women who had similar experiences and fully understood the context of my journey. This common understanding led to a very strong bond among our group.

This inspirational book targets black professional women and others who are open to building cross-cultural relationships. It gives voice to the advancement of women. My hope is that this book will inspire you to:

- Dream big.

- Build and effectively leverage the power of your personal brand.

- Cultivate and maintain positive relationships and friendships that motivate and inspire.

- Break out of the "isolation zone" when you are "the only one."

- Gain insights from master networkers, and adopt them for your own master plan.

- Create a compelling action plan for success regardless of your title or life stage.

- Live your dream!

In addition to networking basics, I've included advice from prominent leaders and executives, many of whom are known for their cross-cultural work. Collectively, I refer to these leaders as the **Networkers Master Class (NMC)**. They have mastered the art of networking, and it is an integral part of how they operate. In the book, these insights are captured as "Lessons from the Masters." Most of the information in these sections came from one-on-one interviews and responses to written surveys.

While some challenges are unique to black women, most successful people have encountered significant hurdles in their ascension into the upper echelons of business. My goal with NMC is to share proven strategies from the experts. Ultimately, you determine what works best for you and which elements you want to include in your personal action plan.

This book is about change. The achievement and maintenance of your dream requires that you take the necessary steps to break out of the status quo. Don't be deterred by naysayers. Make the commitment to yourself today to achieve the life you want and make it happen!

CHAPTER 1

Dare to Dream

Dare to Dream

The biggest adventure you can ever take is to live the life of your dreams.

—Oprah Winfrey

When the newspaper reporter called to ask if I would consider a personal profile story, she told me the title would be "Fulfilling the American Dream." Until that day, I had not thought of my accomplishments in that context. She had done her homework and rattled off a number of awards and contributions, including my role as board president of the largest community action agency in the country, Action for Boston Community Development (ABCD). The timing was a bit awkward. I had recently attended my beloved father-in-law's funeral and was literally on my way to Chicago to represent ABCD at a national antipoverty conference. The photo shoot would have to wait until my return, but I did proceed with the interview.

I have President Barack Obama to thank for the coverage and interest in an immigrant from the island of Barbados. At the time, he was a candidate for president and had defined himself as a community organizer. His candidacy gave rise to visibility of the community action movement. After I spoke with the reporter, the huge newspaper article that followed gave me pause to reflect on my life. Who knew that a poor immigrant girl would reach the heights of her dream and that of her mother's? The story was a reminder that I did have a dream.

As I reflected on my early life in Barbados, West Indies, my mother's words echoed in my ears. While she did not have a formal education, she had a master's degree in emotional intelligence and a doctorate in faith. She would say things like, "We may be poor financially, but we're not poor in spirit. In all your getting, get an education. Hold your head up high. Take pride in how you carry yourself. Dream big; don't let what you see around you define you. I expect the best from you." These powerful words required a huge leap of faith considering we lived in a two-room shack without running water or electricity. Yet her faith was supported by action.

As I look back on the life of my now-deceased mother, she was a consummate networker. She gravitated towards positive people who were doing great things. She was genuinely supportive in helping others advance, even when she did not yet see a way out for herself. She was true to her word and did not let her circumstances define her. As a result, she raised three well-educated daughters, all of whom are carrying the torch to help others improve their lives.

How many times have you heard, "Have a dream," "Live your passion," and "Do what you love"? Easier said than done, right? Sometimes life looks so easy for the people who have "made it." It is as if they had a roadmap and followed it to their dreamland. In reality, success is built one relationship at a time, and I would add success is built one confession at a time. My mother was an example that what we believe and what we speak can become powerful truths when we take positive action. Her faith led her to seek out like-minded people, many of whom helped her to achieve success in life and to create a legacy for her children.

Whether you are trying to advance your career, start or grow your side gig, or increase your personal effectiveness, you are the single biggest influence on your success. I am not denying the challenges that may present themselves in the form of naysayers, limited access to key decision makers, restricted capital, and the big elephant in the room—racism. These are all very real, and the intent here is not to ignore the challenges or to minimize them, but to recognize the common success factor among those who have "made it." They too, experienced hardship, setbacks, and failures of many kinds.

What's different for those who reach the pinnacles of success? They never let go of their dream. They believe deeply in themselves and in their purpose—so much so, that they put in the time and effort required to develop expertise in their fields. When times get tough, they do not give up. Winners continue to plan the work and work their plans. Achievers leverage key skills including networking. Most successful people have mastered the art of developing and maintaining productive relationships with people of all backgrounds and disciplines—and so can you.

In the pages that follow, I will share both strategies and stories of master networkers to help you achieve your dream—whatever that may be for you—and to enhance your effectiveness.

CHAPTER 2

Building and Managing Your Brand

Building and Managing Your Brand

People will judge you by the way you carry yourself. Keep your head held high and take pride in everything you put your hands to do.

—Evelyn C. Clarke

Personal branding is important for any professional but even more so for black women who, by virtue of "social location" tend to have more nuanced professional experiences. Scholars use the term social location to capture how the intersection of gender, race, and social class places a woman in a particular position in society (Bell and Nkomo 2001). Black women often describe barriers as a "concrete ceiling": lack of connection with influential others, lack of informal networks, and lack of opportunity for high-visibility projects (Catalyst 1999).

When it comes to advancement, doing a good job and mastering one's craft are not enough. You need a plan that helps to highlight your value and your contribution. Your personal brand has tremendous impact on how you are perceived by others. Let's face it, achievers want to associate with other successful people—those who have the drive, skills, character, and positive outlook to propel them to even higher heights in their chosen career or business.

Your personal brand is the embodiment of who and what you represent in the minds of others. It is the essence of your emotional, physical, interpersonal, and professional attributes that shapes your reputation and how others view you.

The term "brand" is often associated with physical products and services. Just as images come to mind when you think of CNN, Lexus, Starbucks, Apple, and Google, your name evokes reactions and thoughts from others.

When I think of well-known personal brands, Oprah Winfrey, Maya Angelou, Michelle Obama, Sheila Johnson, and Queen Latifah come to mind. We can learn a lot from these women.

The goal of personal branding is to deliberately influence and shape the thoughts people have about you in ways that will advance your personal, professional, and business agenda.

Be thoughtful and strategic about your actions "live" and in cyberspace. Understand that you cannot control all aspects of how others perceive or receive you; however, you can positively influence those perceptions in most people.

Lessons Learned from the Queen

Queen Latifah is an established celebrity. She is also a wonderful example of a woman whose career has been managed well and a person who has successfully developed and evolved her personal brand.

I first met Queen Latifah in 2007 and had the pleasure of introducing her to three thousand women at the Simmons Women's Leadership Conference. Here is a woman who has reached many pinnacles of success, and she was warm, gracious, and down-to-earth. She was welcoming to everyone she met. I was impressed with her easy personality and quiet confidence. She lived up to her reputation and is a shining example of success for many women regardless of their background. She has embraced change, stayed open to opportunities, and dealt with adversity effectively. She's built and sustained relationships that have helped her through many transitions. As a result, she remains grounded, authentic, relevant, and wildly successful.

What is remarkable about Queen Latifah is the skill with which she has made significant transitions throughout her life and her career. She's gone from a high school basketball talent to rap artist to producer of her own record label and Grammy award–winning artist. From there she went to TV and movies. She's a Cover Girl model. The list goes on. Clearly, hard work, perseverance, and business savvy contributed to her success. She detailed many disappointments, setbacks, and obstacles in her book, *Ladies First: Revelations of a Strong Woman.*

As someone who is working toward effectively creating and/or leveraging social and business networks, you must pay careful attention to your brand. Ultimately, your ability to connect meaningfully with power players at the next level and evolve into an effective networker will rest largely on the strength of your brand.

Each of us has the job of managing our personal brand. It is up to you to take the initiative because the power to change things lies within you. The same principles that gave rise to Queen Latifah's success are available to each one of us and can be used to shape other personal brands. I'll detail some of these next.

Do Great Work

You need to deliver a high-quality product or service. This is a basic requirement for building a strong brand. Whether you are running your own business or working for an organization, don't fall victim to mediocrity.

Guard Your Reputation

Treasure and protect your reputation and your good name offline and online. This is even more important in the age of the Internet and social media. With such quick access to information, it is essential that you carefully manage your image and exposure, as well as the activities and initiatives that become associated with your name.

Take the time to become familiar with commonly used online tools such as LinkedIn, Facebook, or whatever may be the newest tool in your industry or community. Set permissions so that you are protecting the information you do not want to be public. For more on social media, see chapter six, "Winning with Social Media."

Hone Your Positive Attributes

Know your brand attributes. Who are you? If someone were describing you, what are the descriptors you would want them to use? I described Queen Latifah as "warm, gracious, and down-to-earth." Observers may also say that she is talented, humorous, and wealthy. What are your brand attributes? In order to answer this question, you must be self-aware, and you must supplement that with input from others.

Know Your Value

Know your contribution to the market and to your organization. What skills do you bring to the table? What additional value do you add that is a positive differentiator from others? Let's say you are fluent in Creole or Spanish. That is a point of differentiation that can be leveraged to illustrate your worth if your job requires or values linguistic diversity. Articulate your value proposition in a way that enhances your business or work environment. Keep abreast of the market. Know what others are making if they do similar work or provide comparable services. Get a handle on this, and you are in a better position when the time comes to articulate your contributions.

Presence

I'm always struck by the sister who walks into the room and immediately you can tell she is confident, sophisticated, and business savvy. She is well-groomed, wearing a well-cut suit or the appropriate garb. Her posture is good. Judging from her smile, she appears to be approachable. She seems to be at ease with herself and makes others around her comfortable. Girlfriend has presence! Of course, these outward attributes must be accompanied by competence, credibility, and confidence, but you get the picture. You will be judged whether you like it or not. Bring your A-game to the playing field of business by presenting your best self.

Communication

I have a dear friend who is a senior manager at a well-known hospital in the United States. She consistently sent e-mails to me that were casually written and peppered with incorrect grammar and punctuation. Did I mention she is in a senior communications role? I assumed that her lack of attention to grammatical details was due to the casual nature of our exchanges—until she requested a networking introduction. Sarah (not her real name) sent me an e-mail and requested that I forward it to one of my executive contacts along with her resume. I was stunned that the e-mail was casual, poorly written, and lacked punctuation—just like the rest of her casual communiqués.

I started to correct the errors but instead decided to call her and provide her with feedback. She was extremely grateful and sent me a well-written replacement e-mail to accompany her resume. Here is a highly accomplished, talented leader who had fallen into the bad habit of sloppy communications.

Don't continue bad habits. Every e-mail, letter, card, blog, newsletter, voice mail, meeting, and presentation is a reflection of your brand. Communication is a key aspect of networking, so I have dedicated an entire chapter to the topic. See chapter three, "Communicating with Power."

Be Visible

You may have the best products in the world or the best professional contributions in your field. If a great thing happens and no one knows about it, does it have the same impact on society and the world? Imagine if Apple had chosen not to promote the iPod. What if Oprah Winfrey had never aired her shows, her knowledge, and her unique perspective?

The reason we know about high-quality impactful brands is because they were promoted. Notice I did not say *advertised*. While advertising is a paid form of promotion, not everyone has the financial resources of Steve Jobs or Oprah Winfrey—actually, very few do. Promotional opportunities, however, are more accessible. In the business environment they take the form of a memo, a speech, a panel discussion, a keynote presentation, an article, a performance plan, a resume or a networking forum. There are numerous forms of visibility, and you will have to assess what works best for you and your environment.

Don't assume that people know the value of your contribution, product, or service. Seek opportunities to make your work visible to others—updates, presentations, memos, etc.

Again, this is particularly important for black women, who often do not have access to the informal networks or the mentors and sponsors to assist with advancement. See the "Winning with Social Media" and "Strategic and Productive Networking" chapters for low-cost ways to increase your visibility.

Build Brand Equity

Be savvy about managing your image. You are striving to build brand equity and goodwill among your constituents—your associates, shareholders, stakeholders, friends, and equally important, your community. Just as houses build equity through price appreciation and investments that increase the value of the home, personal brand equity is built in the same way.

When you make investments in relationships, improvements in your products and services that increase their value and give back to your community, you are building brand equity.

Give generously. Be helpful. Offer something of value. Volunteer in your community, mentor others, provide quality products and services, and stay true to your word. Not only are these the right things to do, they also help to improve the strength and contribute positive deposits to your professional relationships.

Think of opportunities to give back while getting to know others. That's a win-win.

NMC- Marian L. Heard
President and CEO Oxen Hill Partners
Retired President and CEO
The United Way of Massachusetts Bay and CEO of United Ways of New England
On whether race plays a role in how professionals network:

We cannot say with certainty that race plays a part in determining who is included or who is excluded; however, for those of us who are African American, it is doubly important to indicate your interest and availability for "volunteer" opportunities. Make yourself known within your organization and your community. Join key professional development organizations to meet others who share similar backgrounds or experiences.

Also, make sure that you are connecting to organizations that will provide opportunities to meet with individuals who have *very different* backgrounds and experiences. One of the best ways to do this is to volunteer. I spent over thirty years with the United Way system, the last seventeen in key leadership positions. Also, my other leadership positions were through national nonprofit organizations whose conferences, seminars, and forums provided extensive networking opportunities with key business, entertainment, sports, and political leaders, including the last six U.S. presidents.

Volunteer opportunities should be viewed as a place to address serious social problems and give individuals a platform as well. "Do something good and feel something real" was an early theme for the Points of Light Foundation (now known as the Points of Light Institute), the largest volunteer advocacy and networking group in the world. Groups like this one are excellent vehicles for individuals to give time and money. It feels good to leave each meeting knowing that your efforts have helped those in great need.

Make sure that time is used wisely and that at the end of the day you can say that you made progress with your career and life's goals, but that you also took time to help someone else achieve theirs as well.

Stand Out from the Crowd

Why you? With so many talented business owners, consultants, and executives out there, why would anyone want to network with you, hire you, or buy your products and services? What makes you special?

In order to answer these questions you need to assess where you are and what you have to offer relative to others. In a crowded field of professionals, this is an area that is worthy of your time and attention. Think of this as an analysis of your strengths, weakness, opportunities and threats (commonly known as a SWOT analysis). Then do the same thing for the key people and organizations in the marketplace who you deem to be your competitors, even if you collaborate with them. The point is to identify what makes you different in the context of your peers, other organizations, and services.

Your key points of differentiation should be highlighted in your bio, your company brochure, and in the case of job seekers, your resume. Take a look at the following examples from a fictitious promotional brochure and determine which has key points of differentiation:

This is a new car that can reach up to 150 miles-per-hour, has a little more storage space than usual, and it comes in blue, black, and silver.

The JCMv.7X sets a new standard for innovation, with acceleration from zero to 150 mph in two seconds, unparalleled convenient storage, and your choice of metallic silver, oyster black, or dazzling blue.

Here are two mini bios for women with similar backgrounds. Again, you determine which person has succeeded at differentiating herself.

Armed with a four-year degree, Jan went into the marketing field. She has over twenty-five years of experience and will lead the workshop on how to develop an effective marketing plan.

Jan B. R. Excellente is a nationally recognized marketing expert. A Simmons MBA, Jan created significant buzz when she launched the first JCMv.7X at the 2011 car show. Learn how you too can develop breakthrough marketing plans.

How you describe what you do makes a difference. Be sure to bring out your unique qualities and attributes.

CHAPTER 3

Communicating with Power

CHAPTER 3

Communicating with Power

The way we communicate with others and with ourselves
ultimately determines the quality of our lives.

—Anthony Robbins

Communication is the cornerstone of building a brand, establishing credibility, and building trust. The "how" is as important as the "what" when it comes to communication. In the age of e-communications it is easy to fall into a pattern of rapid responses rather than thoughtful, purposeful exchanges. This chapter provides insights on the "how" for breakthrough communications.

There Goes That Plan Again
Don't be a victim of random communiqués. Have a strategic communications plan for yourself and for your business. Yes, you heard me right. Your personal communications plan consists of ways to market yourself and your value. If this sounds self-promoting, it is. Let's face the facts. Black women often do not have institutional support and when it comes to having access, black women report having "double-outsider" status (Catalyst 2004). While many of our white sisters face similar challenges, the problem is more pronounced for black women, who are more likely to lack access

to mentors, sponsors, and informal networks that could provide a business advantage (Catalyst 2006).

No disrespect to my fellow change agents, but black sisters seem to have a disproportionate number of "D-Suite" and "H-Suite" jobs—diversity, hospitality, and human resources. Don't get me wrong—I've had more than my fair share of these roles and have performed very well, I might add. Often these functions are marginalized, which means that your communication plan becomes even more crucial. Whether you are in a role that may not be valued or are experiencing a lack of support for a business initiative, it is important that you have a powerful communication plan. The plan starts with you.

Communicating with power is one's ability to effectively deliver a message while conveying the essence of your brand through verbal and nonverbal cues.

To maximize your impact, you must carry yourself and interact in a manner that garners respect and one that conveys confidence, competence, and credibility. One's race and gender should not matter but understand that too often "isms" influence perceptions. While there are organizations that do a terrific job in advancing and including women, the reality is that most continue to struggle.

Each person views the world through their lens and a variety of complex filters, which are often unconsciously biased. For black women in the corporate world, there are few visible models of successful women who have reached the upper echelons of the corporate structure. This means that there is a dearth of experience in the corporate world when it comes to dealing with black women in senior leadership positions.

Your interaction, as big or small as you may think, may become the baseline for others—a yardstick by which others are judged, rather fairly or unfairly. It's not necessarily right or wrong; it's life.

The League of Black Women, a not-for-profit organization with a focus on black women leaders, commissioned a study called, "Fostering the Leadership Potential of Black Women in America."

The study found:

> Black women in upper management at corporations are often the first of their race or gender to achieve such status within an organization. Therefore, there are few senior role models and support systems to help black women succeed in the workplace.
>
> Like many women who are first, it is often difficult for black women to find sponsors or mentors at work who can offer constructive guidance and career advancement opportunities. As a consequence, black women often experience isolation and are shut out of important networks that have the potential to enhance their overall professional and personal leadership development.

NMC—Stacy Blake-Beard, Ph.D.
Associate Professor of Management and Faculty Affiliate at the Center for Gender in Organizations
On how networking contributed to her success and the importance of feedback:

> Networking contributed tremendously to every step of my journey. At each career decision that I had to make, I was guided and assisted because somebody was willing to make a call or a connection on my behalf. For example, as I prepare for my trip to India, I am cultivating a relationship with a person with whom I'd like to have a mentoring relationship. I seek advice from her and ask for guidance, which I use to shape my direction and plans. As a mentee, it is important to get multiple perspectives and to be receptive to what people are recommending.
>
> As black women, we tend to put up walls to protect ourselves, and sometimes we do not seek

alternative views. In some cases, we have very good reason to be defensive; however, that defensiveness can hinder the opportunity to get real feedback. It also limits the chance to find alternative ways of doing things, so we miss out, and our organizations miss out too.

Stacy Blake-Beard, Ph.D.
On the role of gender and how professionals network:

There are a number of ways in which gender plays a role—some factors are externally driven while others represent internal processes.

Research shows that women and people of color tend to have bifurcated networks—one network for support and another for advancement. That's a lot of work. We tend to put our heads down and do the work and keep the relationships separate. We need to look up and think about where you're going and not just focus on the work.

Because we are often one of few, we don't necessarily want to call attention to ourselves because of how it might be misinterpreted. Too often we don't ask for help. The fact is that everyone needs help, but there could be a different cost for us. If we ask for help, we could be seen as not as capable while others taking the same actions may be viewed as resourceful. It's a double bind for women in general. For women of color there are additional layers and nuances.

Build Cultural Bridges

For people who have not had an opportunity to build relationships across cultures, it is easy to typecast others, especially when they do not have a positive frame of reference. The absence of visible role models serves to exacerbate the fear and mistrust of others who are not of their same race or ethnicity. Don't feed into the stereotypes. You cannot control what people think and you cannot unilaterally erase the historical baggage or collective corporate experiences; however, you do have the power to influence those with whom you interact.

Use these foundational tools to increase your personal and organizational effectiveness:

Respect

> The fact that the adult American Negro female emerges a formidable character is often met with amazement, distaste, and even belligerence. It is seldom accepted as an inevitable outcome of the struggle won by survivors and deserves respect, if not enthusiastic acceptance.
>
> —Maya Angelou

Respect begins with you. You cannot change the past; however you can influence the present and help to chart a positive course for the future. Congratulations to you if you already have enthusiastic acceptance in the workplace. You are experiencing what many of our sisters are striving to achieve. Kudos to you if you are an entrepreneur who has created an environment and culture of respectful engagement. For the rest of you, read on.

You must focus on what you can control and that means modeling respectful interactions.

Let's start with acknowledging each other. One of the frequent complaints I hear from sisters is about the colleague or leader who does not acknowledge one's presence (you know who they are). This person walks right by you as if you do not exist. They avoid eye contact. They do not speak. In meetings or at social events, they walk into the room and start talking to your peers and totally exclude you from the conversation. Now this is the type of behavior that is difficult to tolerate. You may want to reach for the proverbial "fro" and tell *girlfriend* or *boyfriend* where to go and how to get there quickly! Don't do it! Whether the behavior is conscious or unconscious, you cannot control that person's actions, but you can make it a point to counter that action with a positive one of your own. Try these techniques to turn things around:

- To the colleague who does not acknowledge you in the hallway, say their name and greet him or her with a smile. "Everton, good morning!" Most likely you will jerk the person into consciousness and get a response. You may have to repeat this a few times for them to get the message that it is not okay to walk by you without acknowledging your presence.

- For the person who enters the room at a reception or meeting and speaks to your peers and excludes you, interject yourself into the conversation—with a smile of course. "Everton, glad you could join us!" or whatever phase feels comfortable to you. The point is, you have every right to be in the room or at the table and you need to conduct yourself in a way that reminds others of that fact.

Both of the above scenarios assume positive intent. Most people are not maliciously trying to make your life miserable—no, really. If you are in an environment where these types of positive actions are rebuffed or you experience severe hostility from your colleagues or your superiors on a consistent basis, it's time to consider other options inside and/or outside of your organization. Get out!

Assume Positive Intent

For black women, stereotypes abound. We're too aggressive, too ethnic, too different, too dark, too stylish, too confident, or too much of a loner (that's code for "not a team player"). This baggage will wear you out and negatively impact your psyche if you allow it to mortgage your mind. It's time to foreclose on the negative "toos" and focus on the powerful truths about yourself. In doing so, you can approach each experience from a position of power and exude the beautiful, vibrant attitude of gratitude that God intends for you to have.

If you wonder about a person's motivation, take a step back. Try to give the person the benefit of the doubt and not go to a negative place. Many of our sisters are so beaten down by the daily grind that it is easy to lose sight of the promise that is within all of us. Yes, you too! It is important to be self-aware and to develop your skills. It is equally important to have a vision for yourself and where you want to go. Stay focused on your long-term goal, and don't allow anyone to derail your dreams.

Much of this advice is basic, yet, it is so easy to fall into self-defeating patterns regardless of your level. During challenging periods, assume that others have your best interest at heart, even if they don't. This will help you to focus on positive counteractions and help you to put your energies toward your goals.

When you assume positive motivations and you exhibit uplifting behaviors, most people will respond in kind.

In the previous respect example with Everton, you had a decision to make. Will you speak or not? By smiling and calling that person by name first, you likely received a positive response and subtly brought the behavior to his consciousness. In that example, you neutralized what could have been a spiraling negative trend.

Like it or not, people play games. As you rise higher in the corporate ranks, you are likely to be tested. Sometimes it's simply to see how you will respond to the situation; other times it may be ignorance or discomfort with you.

It's not your job to figure out the motivation of others, but it is your responsibility to act in ways that will build trust and increase your effectiveness.

You must be the change you wish to see in the world.

—Gandhi

You can behave or react to a negative situation, or you can model the behavior that you'd like to see from others. I am not suggesting that everyone walk around with rose-colored glasses. If someone kicks you in the chin and knocks your teeth out, I don't recommend you respond by saying: "It's a wonderful day, and thank you for bashing me in my mouth." But I am suggesting that you realize your power to shape your experiences and not be afraid to use it.

Let's go back to our Everton example. Understand the power of "positive influence," and use it often and generously. When you approach with a smile, it is more likely to break any tension and signal that you are looking for a positive interaction. The bottom line is, even if you strongly believe that someone is not well-intentioned, responding in kind just perpetuates an environment of negativity. Conversely, if you respond from a positive place you are more likely to neutralize the situation—a much more favorable outcome.

Confidence

I heard someone describe First Lady Michelle Obama as statuesque, physically fit, attractive, well dressed, poised, and articulate. She serves as a visible role model for all women—and men for that matter. More importantly, as the first black First Lady, she is helping to positively shift the social consciousness of America and the world. In addition to her appearance, her voice and articulation send a message that this is someone who speaks with authority. She is a woman of conviction and passion.

Like Michelle Obama, most black women have an inner strength and a quiet confidence displayed in social and home settings. You are moms, girlfriends, spouses, partners, teachers, armchair psychologists, sorors, choir members, politicians, community activists, business owners, and expert managers of time.

The issues within organizations can be daunting, but each and every black woman can play a role in helping to bring about change by embracing that same confidence that is left at the corporate threshold and bringing it into the workplace and marketplace.

Establish Your Credibility

You may have your BA, MBA, Ph.D., JD, or some other designation, but credentials do not equal credibility. Unfortunately, the societal issues that blacks face do not end with the crossing of the threshold of the office or workplace. Too often, there is an extra hurdle applied to people who are different—whether it is gender, age, sexual orientation, or race. In many cases, they are forced to "prove" they belong.

It is imperative that you assume nothing and find ways to let the key players know about your capabilities. You can weave this into conversations without being overly boastful or by placing your awards and diplomas in your office or business space. Ideally, you want the information to come from multiple sources, so the burden is not just on you talking about yourself. Share key information, speaking engagements, and forums you are leading with your business associates. These things serve as a reminder that you are a player in the business community. Ultimately, it is your responsibility to track and communicate your accomplishments.

NMC—Cheryl Ginyard-Jones
Managing Principal – Energy & Utilities, Verizon Business
On adding value and sharing knowledge:

> Make sure you focus on adding value to your organization. Develop one or two areas where you are the go-to person so that you can demonstrate your value to the organization. Proving that you are a strong contributor may increase your value to your organization or will help you find a new job more quickly.

Make sure you stay current in your field and that you know the latest trends. The more insights you can provide to the organization, the more you will be able to help them deliver. Find opportunities to share your knowledge and insights. You can write a blog or a white paper, or be presenter at conferences and professional meetings.

Communicate with Impact—High Impact Tips

Approach your communications with a high degree of professionalism.

E-mails

Use proper punctuation and capitalization in your professional e-mails. How you communicate online with your friends is your business; however, your communication in business and in the workplace is a reflection on you and your brand.

Speaking and Presentations

Seek opportunities to present and to speak, both at internal meetings and external forums. The discipline, skill, and oral communication used for presentations will serve you well and raise your visibility. Prepare for your speech or presentation; please do not read your speech word-for-word. Ideally, you should commit it to memory and use prompts or key phrases to jog your memory. If you are pressed for time or memorization is not feasible due to the length or complexity of your speech, at least read your prepared remarks out loud prior to giving your talk and build in pauses so that you are periodically looking at your audience. Make sure you present with passion.

NMC—Bobby Rodriguez
Chief Diversity Officer, Bay State Health
Observations on communication styles:

Understand how men communicate. Men are generally not multitaskers. Men tend to be linear thinkers. Women tend to be multitaskers, and this is often seen in communication styles. When women present to groups, it is important to do so in ways that will resonate with men. Complex messages need to be translated to linear thinking. This does not mean that women need to act like men, but it is important to be aware of the gender influences on communication. Women who master this seem to do very well. Lastly, maintain your professional standards and be true to who you are as a woman.

Meetings

Prepare for meetings as you would a presentation, regardless of your role. If you are leading the meeting, take time to think through the role of the participants and their interests. Be clear about your objectives and that of your participants. Send an agenda in advance of the meeting. Respect the time of your colleagues and participants by starting and ending the meeting as scheduled.

If you are playing the role of participant, read the agenda and think through your contribution to the meeting. Actively engage by listening carefully to the discussion. Ask thoughtful questions. Pay attention to your body language and your facial expressions. You want to convey interest, not boredom. Be sure to follow up on any action items after the meeting. Your primary objective should be to add value.

Connecting with Your Audience and Colleagues

Every day you have an audience, whether it's coworkers, subordinates, other executives, or mentees. Put yourself in their shoes and ask the basics: who, what, where, when and how, relative to interpersonal connections. Collaborate and create an environment that makes others feel comfortable connecting with you. Again, you play the role of educator. I know what you're thinking: *Why is it that we always have to be the ones educating others and helping them feel comfortable?* This is a fair question and one that is frequently posed to me given the nature of my professional work. Having championed the diversity agenda for most of my career both formally and informally, I know this is a sensitive topic. Rather than viewing it as a burden, look at it as an opportunity to influence change.

Many blacks still have "token status," often the only ones in their particular group, leadership team, or boardroom. Introduced by Rosebeth Moss Kanter, this concept of token theory is defined as "the few of a different type in an organization with a numerically dominant type" (Bell and Nkomo 2001).

While Kanter's theory does not specifically address race, this dynamic is very real for black women. A common fear is that other employees might assume black women are given preferential treatment, and therefore we aren't truly qualified.

This notion of meaningful connection is incredibly important in the work and business environment; it is essential. As I alluded to previously, the burden is on you to establish credibility, reach out to colleagues, and to strengthen your emotional intelligence in order to advance your professional agenda. See chapter eight for more on "the only one."

Take Inventory and Take Action!

Now is the best time to start or modify your approach to powerful communications. Take assessment of your "how." Once you have answered the questions, identify where your gaps are and add them to your personal development plan.

- Are you presenting yourself as someone who should be taken seriously?

- Are you establishing relationships across cultures, generations, and diverse industries?

- Are you building bridges or putting up walls? Are you engaging in ways that are respectful of others?

- Do you acknowledge your colleagues in the hallway, or are you so self-absorbed that you don't speak?

- Do you assume positive intent when a perceived slight occurs?

- Do your clothing, voice, posture, and manner convey confidence?

- Do you communicate your accomplishments to the appropriate people?

- Are your e-mails professional—well written, punctuated, and appropriate for the business environment?

- Do you seek opportunities to present your work and ideas? If so, are you prepared?

- Are your meetings substantive and well structured? Do you have an agenda, stated objectives, and the right participants and contributors?

- Are you connecting with your audience?

CHAPTER 4

Strategic and Productive
Networking

CHAPTER 4

Strategic and Productive Networking

Networking is the process of cultivating mutually beneficial relationships that increase visibility and expand
opportunities.

—J. Keith Motley, Ph.D.

Networking can be time-consuming. In order to increase your
effectiveness, you must create or tap into networks that are
both strategic and productive. Ultimately, you want to spend your
time on those activities that will get you closer to your goals, while
developing and sustaining relationships that are mutually beneficial.

Strategic networking requires development of a plan with
actionable goals. Not all contacts have equal value. Not everyone
will align themselves with the objectives that you are trying to
accomplish.

You may be thinking, *Just where am I supposed to find the time
for this additional work?* After all, there is just so much energy
to go around. And you're right. If you're like most professional
women, you are already operating at, near, or beyond capacity.
The beauty of a strategy that you are passionate about is that it
forces prioritization and realignment. You become energized by
the clarity of purpose—strategic focus. This means that you must
learn to say no to low-value or no-value activities that do not align

with your goals and yes to high-priority action items that move you towards your objectives.

Stratify and manage your network. Here is my model for being effective at strategic networking. There are numerous ways of looking at this, so find a framework that works for you and modify it to meet your needs.

Strategic Networking Model:

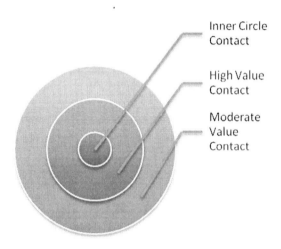

Inner Circle
Contact

High Value
Contact

Moderate
Value
Contact

Inner Circle Contacts (ICC)—Small in number and highly influential

ICCs are people with whom you have a deep trusting relationship that has stood the test of time. You can discuss highly sensitive subjects with them and know that your conversation will be confidential. They care about you and have been there for you through the tough times. They are your cheerleaders and bring opportunities to you. They provide access to places and resources. These are your advisors, mentors, and friends who truly have your best interest at heart. They know your goals and dreams and support them whole-heartedly. They have nominated you for awards, provided references, counseled you those times when you were stuck, and generously given of their time to help you succeed. They are authentic, and they give you constructive feedback and encouragement as needed.

Managing your ICC Network:

- Treasure and nurture these relationships. Do not take them for granted.

- Actively think about how you can be helpful to them and conduct random acts of kindness.

- Be sincere and authentic in your dealings.

- Praise them, and use them as examples in forums where it would be beneficial to their business.

- Refer business to them.

- Recommend them for speaking engagements (for those who speak).

- Share your vision and goals with them. Schedule time to connect with them in-person at least two times a year, and maintain contact throughout the year via e-mail, periodic calls, and letters. Forward information that may be of interest to them.

- Extend invitations to important events.

- Return their calls immediately.

High Value Contact (HVC)—Larger pool of contacts than ICC and high degree of influence

HVCs are people with whom you have a trusting relationship. You may have worked with them for many years. Perhaps you went to college with them or sat on a board together. They may be sorors or attend the same church. HVCs respect you, and you have very good rapport with them. You share information and resources, and they know enough about you to provide a job or business reference. There is mutual respect.

The relationship is not as deep as your inner circle; however, these are people you can count on as professionals, colleagues, and friends. They "have your back."

Managing Your HVC Network:

- The management of HVCs is very similar to ICCs; however, ICCs have a higher prioritization when it comes to your time and the level of information shared.

Moderate Value Contact (MVC)—Largest pool of contacts with potential for advancing to a higher tier.

MVCs are people with whom you have a connection. It may have come from a networking event, a business forum, your child's school, or a conference. For MVCs, the relationship may be relatively new, or you may have known the person for years, but your goals and interests do not necessarily align. You may have mutual respect but don't necessarily have the depth of relationship where you would put your professional reputation on the line for that person. Your goal with MVCs is to stay connected; however, you are not to invest the same level of time and effort as you would for your HVC or ICC contacts.

There is still value in your MVC network and there may be occasional opportunities for you to lend support for an initiative that does not have a high risk to your reputation.

Managing Your MVC Network:

- Use electronic communications to maintain visibility and touch-points with your MVCs.

- Use e-introductions such as e-mail, LinkedIn, and text messages to connect MVCs to each other.

- Be sparing in your use of prime venues such as luncheons and dinners. Carefully evaluate invitations that will suck up your time and do not have a clear objective.

- There may be times when an ICC requests that you meet with an MVC. In this instance, you should accommodate the request.

I've discussed three networking tiers: Inner Circle Contacts, High Value Contacts, and Moderate Value Contacts. You may be wondering about the fourth tier—Low Value Contacts. By definition, when you are operating strategically, it is not a good use of your time to connect with people for the sake of connecting. I know some will disagree with me, but we are talking about "strategic and productive networking." Implicit in this concept is the idea that you will align your resources, time, and energy to the things that matter most. It also means managing your plan in ways that will maximize your effectiveness and support your goals. For this reason, I will leave it to others to address categories beyond the three that I have identified.

Networking tiers are not static, and neither is your plan, so it is entirely possible for an MVC to evolve to an HVC and vice versa.

Laying the Groundwork for Your Networking Plan

You should start with developing or refining your business or career plan and then overlaying your networking plan.

Let's start with the plan for your side-gig, which you hope to grow into your main livelihood:

Start with your vision and goals—Envision the future for you and your business. Imagine that you are on the cover of *Black Enterprise* magazine five years from now, and it is a very positive story about your business. What would be the headline? What would the photographs look like? What accomplishments would the writers tout? Take the time to reflect on where you want to take your business.

Let's say your vision for your side gig is to grow your business to be the premier technology company for businesses in Chicago.

To do this, you have a set of goals that include:

- Achieve $2 million in revenue by 2014 through targeted focus on high-growth STEM (Science, Technology, Engineering and Math) companies

- Evaluate at least four partnership opportunities each year, and implement at least one to accelerate profitable growth of the business

- Complete modification of IT architecture by end of 2012 to ensure flexible, scalable options for larger clients and to maximize future acquisition opportunities

While your vision is grand, as it should be, your goals are S.M.A.R.T.—Specific, Measurable, Attainable, **and** Realistic, with Timeframes attached.

Strategies to Increase Visibility—Staying with our technology example, here are a few of the things that you've done to raise your company's visibility in the business community.

- You are a member of the Chamber of Commerce

- You attend and speak at leading STEM conferences

- You provide thought leadership by writing articles

- Your vendor nominated you for a "Best Company" award, and your company won. You sent the press release out to all of your clients; posted the honor on your company's website, LinkedIn profile, and Facebook page; and you've updated your bio and executive communications to make note of the honor. *By the way, great picture of you in* Black Enterprise *magazine. You go, girl!*

Networking to Grow Your Business

You are well on your way to advancing your business objectives, so how can you be more strategic? It's time to rev up your strategic networking plan.

As you gain influence and visibility, more people will place demands on you. You must have a laser-like focus on your goals and your time commitments. It is time to zero in on the high-value networking activities such as those noted earlier in this chapter. This does not mean dismissing or disrespecting other relationships; it just means that you spend most of your time and energy on those activities that are likely to yield high returns.

Leverage the relationships that you have established to access the inner circle of the decision makers and movers and shakers with whom you want to connect. Well, this all sounds great, but how does one do this? Ask.

NMC—Josefina Bonilla
President, Color Media Group LLC and publisher of Color Magazine
Advice to women:

> Don't be afraid to ask for help. Find a select group of allies who provide you with a zone where you can be vulnerable to seek advice and support. In addition to networking, you have to keep learning. Come from a place of interest. It is important to be open to other professionals and what they do. You must listen, listen, listen.

NMC—Jackie Glenn
Chief Diversity Officer, EMC
On Women's Advancement:

> Do a good job even if you are not recognized for your work. Don't skimp or cut corners. Do something that you are passionate about. If you hate what you're doing, find another job. When it comes to advancement, you have to ask. To get what you want, you have to get comfortable with making the request. Rarely will you be handed anything.

Mastering "The Ask"

Let me be clear! As a proud, black, West Indian woman, learning how to ask for help did not come easy for me. For many of my black sisters and brothers, pulling oneself up by one's own bootstraps is a familiar expression. Another popular saying is that those of us who have achieved any level of success stand on the shoulders of our ancestors. Self-sufficiency, self-reliance, resilience, and pride are attributes that most of my friends and family embrace.

Asking for what you want means that you are relying on others to meet a need, and there is some level of dependency involved. For some, this may signal a deficiency or vulnerability. I discuss this more in chapter eight, "The Only One."

For right now, let's look at this concept as a strategic asset and focus on how to ask in ways that will advance your business.

Be Clear About Your Ask

Let's go back to our technology example. You now have the ear of the CIOs for some of the largest STEM companies, and this is your second meeting with the chair of the Technology Council, Gina Danvers (not her real name). She was impressed with the presentation that you gave at the chamber, and her actions have led you to believe that she is sincere in wanting to help small businesses.

You must now seize the moment, but before doing so, determine exactly what your request will be. This is not the time for vague objectives such as, "I want to grow my business." Of course you do. You need to articulate to Gina how she can help your company. Are you looking for a referral, an endorsement, a contract bid, technical assistance, industry advances, or board members recruitment for your company?

Narrow your focus, and be prepared to say why your company is unique. What makes you different from the other businesses? Why do you think you can actually achieve your revenue targets in the timeframe that you have set for yourself? What specific support is essential to expedite your growth?

Perhaps you have a patent for a new technology that you plan to license, and you are looking to obtain expert advice in this area. You may also need some board members with specific expertise to help guide your company through this next phase. Whatever you need, crafting your story and making "the ask" are more likely to get you results.

Practice your message, but do not deliver a rote, over-rehearsed script. You must display sincerity, positive energy, and confidence. Make your request powerful and succinct.

Address W.I.I.F.H.

Make sure you know Gina's priorities and her business challenges. She will be even more receptive if you can tie her interests to your interests. As a leader, you must also think through the W.I.I.F.H., a variation on "What's in it for me?" In this instance, W.I.I.F.H. represents "What's in it for her (or him)?" The concept is a means of examining the interests of the person you are trying to influence. Admittedly, this process can be a little intimidating, right?

In our example, Gina is the guru/industry giant, and you represent the newer technology company looking for growth opportunities. This means that getting to the W.I.I.F.H. will require some work on your part. Do your research. Talk to others who know Gina. Read industry publications that reference her. Google her! What are the things that would help her succeed in advancing her agenda?

Lead with W.I.I.F.H.

Always start with the other party's agenda before asking for help. What is Gina looking to accomplish during her tenure as chair of the council? Let's say her number one priority is to bring more young people to the technology sector, or perhaps she wants to increase the membership within the council and ensure that it is more diverse in terms of race and gender.

How can you utilize your expansive network to help Gina achieve her goals? Is there a creative way that you can leverage your contact with historically black colleges to establish a program and pipeline for black students to gain exposure to the industry through internships and sponsorship? Perhaps you can arrange a forum for Gina to meet with the key influencers.

Ideally, your strategic ask will be compelling, as it would help Gina solve a problem and position your company for success at the same time.

What If The Power Scales are Skewed?

You may not always be in a position to offer something of equal significance to the person from whom you seek help. You should still ask about their challenges and priorities and try to identify the W.I.I.F.H. If you are unable to do so, don't fret about it. Be sincere in your offer to help, and let the person know that you want them to call on you when an opportunity should arise to help them. This goes a long way. Just be prepared to prioritize their request when the time comes.

Do what you can. Refer business, send information that may be of value, invite them to exclusive events when appropriate, talk up their initiatives in your speeches, and provide unsolicited endorsements for their work. Execute random acts of kindness. The small deeds can sometimes add more value than you may think. Lastly, but most importantly, say thank you. Acknowledge the help that you have received, and make it a point to let the person know the impact of their actions.

NMC—Paul Guzzi
President and CEO, Greater Boston Chamber of Commerce
On the keys to growth and advancement:

There are multiple factors that contribute to success including a certain amount of luck and timing. One of the keys to growth and advancement is doing an outstanding job. As one's career develops, formal and informal networks can be very helpful.

Work hard. Work smart. There is no substitute for hard work. Develop, build, and expand your networks. It's as much about what you can give as about what you can take.

No one formula fits everyone in every situation. It is important that you be yourself. Don't try to be someone you're not. Authenticity is important. Develop confidence in who you are and what you have to give. Be persistent in terms of fulfilling career and business aspirations—it's an important quality.

Strategic Career Management

What on earth is strategic career management? By now, you may have noticed the theme that planning is an essential part of effective strategic networking. That doesn't mean you're doomed if you don't have a plan. A plan just makes your job less challenging.

How many times have you gotten a call from a long-lost friend seeking assistance with finding a job and the conversation goes like this. (*Names have been changed for the purpose of this illustration.*)

Scenario 1: "Jen, it's Meg Marchelle calling. It's good to reconnect with you. I'm so sorry I haven't kept in touch over the past ten years. I know you reached out to me on a number of occasions, but girl, you know how things are..."

Jen thinks*: So she did get the e-mails and was just too busy to hit the "reply" button to acknowledge the e-mail.*

Meg: "...I'm actually looking for a job and I'm hoping that you can connect me to Janet at Forever Prosperous Inc. I saw a picture of the two of you in the news clips, and you looked great. Would you mind setting up an introductory lunch so that I can meet Janet?"

Jen thinks*: So, why would I want to go the extra mile and leverage my relationship with Janet for Meg, who did not have the courtesy of responding to my communications over the past ten years?*

Here's another favorite, a reference request:

Scenario 2: "Hi, Jen. I'm Jonathan Bizkid and I'm calling from Productive Resources Inc. Joanne Wonderful gave your name as a reference for a position here in the marketing division. She is one of two finalists, and I'd appreciate if you would give me a call back within the next few days or complete the form I sent you and return it to me by e-mail at jbizkid@proresourcesinc.com. My number is (555)444-1234. Jen, thanks in advance for your prompt attention to this matter. I know the form is a little long, but I hope you will give me your candid assessment of Joanne."

Jen thinks: *I didn't have the first clue that Joanne Wonderful used me as a reference. Furthermore, I don't know her work well enough to vouch for her or complete this four-page form. You would think that she would have asked my permission before using me as a reference. Marketing? I thought all of her experience was in geology. Interesting. I would shoot her an e-mail, but I haven't spoken to her in so long, I'm not even sure if I have her contact information.*

In both scenarios, the requests required an investment of time and resources from Jen.

In the first scenario, Meg's issue is a very common one. She is very talented, but she has taken her relationship with Jen for granted and has not been strategic about managing her network. She is treating Jen as a HVC, yet she has not invested in the relationship. Meg has not given Jen the courtesy of a return e-mail, call or card, but now she is asking Jen to use her highly valued contact for her benefit.

In the second scenario, Joanne has provided Jen's name as a reference, something that should not be taken lightly. Many organizations use third parties to verify a candidate's background and provide further insights about her qualifications.

All other things being equal, a strong, well thought-out reference could make all the difference in securing the position. You may be thinking that it's just common sense that you would ask someone before listing them as a reference. Many people don't ask first. For those who do, you want to make sure that you brief the person on the position. Provide an updated copy of your resume, and highlight the key attributes about the job as it relates to your skill set. In other words, don't make Jen do the work. You have an opportunity to make the process seamless, which can have a positive influence on her responses. Without arming Jen with the background information, Joanne may miss out on her marketing opportunity.

Stay Connected to ICCs and HVCs

Whether you are considering a career change or simply are looking to maximize options for advancement, make it a point to stay connected with ICCs and HVCs.

Relationships are complex and nuanced; they need to be nurtured. This is true for familial networks, business alliances, and partnerships. Building and maintaining productive relationships require deliberate actions that will build your brand, support your personal and professional objectives, and provide mutually rewarding experiences.

NMC—Helen Drinan
President and CEO, Simmons College
On the importance of leveraging your brand to increase your networking effectiveness:

Your strategy will likely be more successful if you have developed a strong personal brand. Develop your own personal brand. Think of yourself as a product to be managed, advertised, developed, and sold. At a certain point, we have to understand the competition and find ways to differentiate ourselves. It can't just be bravado. You have to be willing to put yourself out there and take opportunities to speak in public or write for an association magazine.

- Get known as an authority in your own right.

- You can get really invested inside the organization. Don't stay inside too long. You need to see and be seen by the outside world.

- Be very clear about your long-term goals, and arrange your short-term goals with those in mind.

- Stay true to your dreams and work towards those. Take it in "bites."

- Stay attentive to where you fit within the organization and in your job.

- Take advantage of opportunities for public appearances and conferences that are relevant in your field.

- Attend at least two or three charity events per year.

- Take the initiative to start a new role if you have outgrown your job. Don't stay too long in one role.

Helen's advice reminds us of the importance of having clear goals and providing specific action steps for enhancing networking effectiveness.

CHAPTER 5
Networking Action Plan

Networking Action Plan

If you don't know where you're going, any road will get you there.

—Lewis Carroll

Thinking through the elements of your strategic networking plan is the first part of the process. Next, you need to document your plan. Write it down, and it is more likely to get done. I have no idea who said this originally, but I wholeheartedly agree with this concept. In this chapter I will walk you through development of your networking plan.

As we discussed in chapter four, you should share your plan with your inner circle contacts (ICCs), as they are your strongest allies. Beyond your ICCs, be selective when sharing your plans. In her book *The Complete Leader*, Marian Heard notes, "Everybody doesn't love you, and everybody doesn't want you to succeed." Spend your time with those who have your best interest at heart.

As part of your planning process, schedule time to review your plan at least twice a year. I highly recommend the buddy system to help you stay on track. Find a friend with similar ambitions, and create and review your respective plans together. My friend Martha and I have done this for many years. At least twice a year, the two of us retreat from the hustle and bustle of work, community commitments, and family obligations to discuss and review our plans. We have very candid conversations about what is working well and what could use some changes. We also have fun by scheduling our review around fun activities such as lunch at a nice restaurant or prior to an elegant event. In doing so, this important work of assessing and reviewing one's strategic roadmap doesn't feel like drudgery.

By monitoring and reviewing your goals, you are more likely to stay on track.

Creating and Documenting Your Plan

On a separate sheet of paper, write responses to each of the following questions:

1) What is your vision for yourself and your business? Think five to ten years out.

2) What are your values—those non-negotiable principles by which you live and govern your life?

3) What are your goals? Think about all dimensions of your life, as they are interconnected. You may find it helpful to create goals and sub-goals for each of the major categories that you value:

   a. Health

   b. Family

   c. Spiritual

   d. Financial

   e. Business and Career

   f. Community and Politics

Make sure your goals are S.M.A.R.T.E.R.: Specific, Measurable, Action-oriented, Realistic, Time-bound, Ethical, and Resourced (Source: www.achieve-goal-setting-success.com).

4) What are your top priorities? If you were forced to pick no more than five goals, what would they be?

5) How are you currently spending your time relative to your goals and priorities? How much time do you spend on non-core activities (those activities that do not support your goals)?

6) Are your activities and commitments aligned with your personal and professional objectives?

7) Are you making progress towards your longer-term goals?

8) What metrics do you have in place to assess progress?

9) Do you have a networking strategy? If so, is it aligned with your goals and objectives—both short- and long-term?

10) What changes should you make to increase the effectiveness of your networking?

11) How have you contributed to advancing your community?

12) Are your personal and professional relationships productive? Are you spending time with the right people?

Time to Work Your Plan

There's a reason it's called networking. Work is at the center of an effective plan.

> Networking is a vehicle to develop relationships. You have to work at it. Maintaining your relationships and updating your database is work you need to do to sustain your network. Out of sight, out of mind.
>
> —Martha R. A. Fields

We're all running at 100 miles an hour. Who has time to develop a plan, manage a database, and reach out to other people? Isn't it hard enough trying to keep up with the basic necessities—delivering at work, church, community, and side gig?

It's time to change your thinking. While there is work involved with networking, you're already doing a lot of the activities. You just have to approach them differently.

Now that you have prioritized your goals, pick your top five and think about your existing relationships. Identify activities that will deepen key relationships. Brainstorm ways to sustain and grow your network in ways that will support executing on your goals.

Getting Started:

Step 1: Engage in at least one networking activity per week.
Instead of wolfing down lunch at your desk while you check e-mails and read reports, what if you dedicated at least one day a week to having lunch with a colleague or someone in a different industry you would like to get to know better? Just this one change (if done on a consistent basis) will substantially expand your network. Your plan can be that simple.

Step 2: Tier your network.
Stratify your existing contacts into ICC, HVC, and MVC (discussed in chapter four). Approach your stratification with your prioritized goals in mind.

Step 3: Identify key networking opportunities or create your own outreach.
Check out available networking opportunities in your industry and within your organization. Don't overlook the ones that are already within reach such as those on community boards on which you serve. Research taskforces and conferences.

Target at least one networking event per month. Ideally, you should have one professional or industry membership for your business or organizational affiliation. Before attending events and forums, do your homework. Determine who will be in attendance—which organizations, consultants, influencers, and vendors you should connect with at the event. Establish some objectives for your attendance and/or participation.

- What do you wish to accomplish while you are there?
- What would success look like? Write it down.

Leverage the power of search engines to enhance your networking prowess. Use Google or another search engine to research speakers and known attendees in advance of the session. The information you learn could then be used to spark an informed conversation. Most people love to talk about themselves and their accomplishments. By doing your homework, you will be in a better position to have a deeper connection beyond the general name and title exchange.

NMC—Martha R. A. Fields
President and CEO, Fields Associates Inc.
On the value of professional organizations:

> Getting to know people in professional organizations was key. I found that becoming active on a board was a good way to get involved. I was very active on the board of The Boston Human Resources Association. Through that organization, I got to know a lot of entrepreneurs. When I got to the point of starting my own business, I had the relationships and sounding boards to assess whether I should proceed. Ultimately, this helped me to make a career choice and solidified my decision.

Step 4: Create a financial plan.

This is a very important component of your plan. Without the funding, your dream will not be realized. Get your financial house in order, and establish a budget. For example it may take twenty-four networking luncheons (two per month) or coffees for your entrepreneurial pursuits to be sustained. The person who makes the invitation generally picks up the tab, so factor these and other costs such as conferences, dinners, communications, business supplies, airfare, etc. into your budget. Research the costs of your plan, and identify the appropriate funding sources. You don't want your fabulous dream to turn into a financial nightmare!

Start small. If you don't have the funding just yet, look for free events and networking meet-ups. Leverage online resources such as Frasernet.com, Kscopecity.com, and other business news sources to stay plugged in as you work towards strengthening your financial position.

Step 5: Expand your "known" quotient.

It's okay to start with people you know, but the productivity of your network will come from "who knows you." It is quite possible that you have a substantial contact list of people you have met over the course of your career. How many of those people actually know you well enough to be able to vouch for you or recommend you? Do they really know you as a person? Do they know your capabilities? Your objective should be to focus on being known to the people who are core to your strategy. When you increase the number of people who really know you and your outstanding work, they can become your ambassadors, cheerleaders, and in some cases, your ICCs.

Step 6: Diversify your network.

Many of us tend to have much stronger ties within our own race when it comes to networking, socializing, and religious affiliations. There is a saying that Sunday mornings are the most segregated time in the week. Get to know people who are different from you. In our increasingly global world, these relationships will be a source of strength.

To be an effective networker in this evolving world, you must increase your comfort zone. This can be done by:

- Making it a point to include people from different backgrounds, races, ethnicities, ages, and genders in your inner circle. This process takes time; you won't be able to check it off your list in a day. It requires being consciously and deliberately inclusive.

- Acting as a convener among influential people. In Vernon Jordan's memoir, *Vernon Can Read*, one of the things that struck me was his commentary about inviting others and not always being the one to be invited. While this might seem like a small thing, there is significant power in being the convener, particularly when it comes to business and career transactions.

The opportunities for convening people are plentiful. You can do this during the course of your workday by seeking input from others, facilitating dialogues, or hosting a substantive meeting. Don't meet for the sake of meeting. By bringing people together, you have an opportunity to influence the agenda and accelerate connections among your constituents while positively building your brand. This is true on the social side as well. It can be a lot of fun to go to the homes of friends and attend birthday parties, dinners, and social clubs. You get to skip the expense and the clean up. Yes! You may not be in a position to reciprocate in similar fashion, but do find a way to include those who consistently extend themselves in a venue of your own. It could be at a restaurant, picnic, gospel concert, or whatever fits your style and your budget. The point is to move from receiver to giver and convener.

Step 7: Be proactive in your outreach.

Once you have identified the people with whom you want to connect, reach out to them in advance of the session. You can do this via e-mail, or send a card or handwritten note. Despite the popularity of online technology, a brief handwritten letter (that includes your contact information) sent through snail mail is often more impactful. It is a subtle message that you are someone who has taken the time, effort, and forethought to reach out. Understand that the rapid pace of business has placed a significant strain on professionals and leaders. Although well intended, you may not get a response or acknowledgement of your communication. Gone are the days of leaders surrounded by layers of administrative support and assistants to return the long list of calls. Whether or not you get a response, you have increased your brand equity by adding to the positive impression of your professional brand. With this simple gesture, you have already separated yourself from the pack.

Step 8: Add value.

Think of common interests or potential ways in which you can strike a win-win connection. Ideally, you want to identify something that will help to advance your business and or career while supporting the goals and objectives of the person with whom you are trying to build a relationship. Don't worry if the exchange is not mutually beneficial; not every connection will be equal. However, you should strive for this goal whenever possible. Here is an example of a note you can send to introduce yourself prior to meeting:

Dear Juliette:

Congratulations. I read the recent article in the *Patriot Ledger*, "Fulfilling the American Dream," and was so inspired by your personal journey. As an entrepreneur and aspiring author, I look forward to your upcoming presentation on networking at the Simmons Women's Leadership Conference.

Warm Regards,
Vernice Z. Triy
President, Phenomenal Events

With this simple note, Vernice has accomplished several things:

1. In a nonintrusive way, she has introduced herself to Juliette. No response requested. No "ask" with the first introduction.

2. She has given Juliette a heads-up that she will be at the upcoming conference.

3. Vernice took the time to find out something about Juliette. This gesture can be quite flattering to the recipient.

4. She has also introduced her company, Phenomenal Events.

5. Vernice has made a positive deposit to her personal brand equity account.

The "How" of Networking for Black Women

Avoid the "Angry Black Woman" Label

Have you ever sat in a meeting and heard something like this? "John is decisive, clear about his purpose, and assertive. He gets results."

On the other hand when a woman exhibits similar behavior, she is often labeled as angry: "She has a chip on her shoulder." When it's a black sister, well, there goes the angry black woman.

As you move through new circles, be sensitive to the realities that may play out; however, push through the slights and do your part to bridge the divide.

Behaviors that may be acceptable for men or even our white sisters are often interpreted very differently for women of color. An executive friend of mine recalled her peer being praised for pushing back and going toe-to-toe with the guys; however, when she exhibited similar behavior, she was called angry and overly sensitive. I share this not to disparage white men or women, as many of them are with us in the struggle for a place at the table. The reality is that racial stereotypes often play into the reactions that people have towards people of color.

In addition to the socio-professional challenges that white women confront on a daily basis, black women have additional layers and social nuances—namely that of race. I believe it's incumbent upon all women to speak up when these types of disparities occur.

In his book *Microaggressions in Everyday Life*, Dr. Derald Wing Sue examines many of the daily slights that people of color endure. It is important not to obsess about the slights but to keep focused on the productive relationships that will move you towards your goals.

Keep Your Word

Do what you say you're going to do. If you can't, follow up with your contact and let them know why *before* you are late delivering on your commitment.

In the workaday world that we live in, it is easy for some people to let things slide. Your word is a test of your brand's strength.

Have you ever purchased a product or service where you were lavished with attention and praise before the sale? The sales person made you feel like a million bucks. Their promise, however, was not fulfilled because the equipment broke not long after you got it home. You called the sales representative and customer service repeatedly. After many wasted hours and lack of follow-up, you gave up or wrote a letter to the sales person expressing your disappointment and asking for her assistance. No response.

Would you purchase another product from that sales representative? Would you refer your friends? No. Absolutely not! The trust and the brand equity are gone. Don't let this happen to you. When you make commitments to your network, keep your word.

Venture into New Territory

Even for seasoned professionals, networking beyond your comfort zone can be daunting. If you are uncomfortable going to a new venue, take a friend. Also, identify networking opportunities that are likely to attract diverse people. Your plan should include a variety of venues. While you may be outside of your comfort zone, do not give up without a sustained effort to build new relationships.

NMC—Colette A.M. Phillips
President and CEO, Colette Phillips Communication and
Founder of Get Konnected
On cross-cultural innovations:

Get Konnected is the largest multicultural networking forum in Boston, Massachusetts. Eight years prior to starting Get Konnected, I created Kaleidoscope, the first multicultural directory in Boston for professional, personal care, and business resources. By working with many of the affinity groups in Boston, I realized that there was a need to bring diverse groups together. Originally, Get Konnected was a social experiment to address some of the social challenges. It is a free, professional networking event open to all cultures. It is not intended to replace affinity groups, as these groups still serve a very important role for professionals.

NMC—Edie Fraser
Edie Fraser, Senior Consultant, Diversified Search
On the value of networking:

> Networking is the ultimate for achieving success in business. It is everything—particularly in executive search. The contacts and relationships are critical. I think of it as contacts to contracts. I've had networking relationships turn into solid friendships where people are there to listen, support, and go the extra mile. It is a huge contributor to my success.

Be Prepared

Even if your business is small, you should have a summary and marketing brochure that describes your capabilities. You should also have a professional bio that summarizes your key accomplishments. You should have this ready before it is requested. It is a lot easier to update it than to start from scratch. You can find helpful templates at www.writeabio.com.

From a career standpoint, there are actually people who get jobs purely through networking and often times they are not required to submit a resume. Not everyone is that fortunate, so don't assume this will apply to you. Regardless of your career stage, it is important to keep your resume updated. It's also a good idea to have a one pager that summarizes your professional accomplishments such as a bio. Your bio should be in good shape and ready to go should the opportunity for a speaking engagement, award nomination, or a networking opportunity arise.

Be Authentic

Authenticity means not hiding who you are. I've had friends scrub their resumes and bios to remove any trace of anything that may potentially reveal their ethnicity. While I understand wanting to tailor one's resume for the particular opportunity, you should assess whether you really want to work for an organization or leader who is offended by your race or ethnicity. You want to go where you will be celebrated, not just tolerated!

Plan Your Meetings and Calls

Just as you would not walk into an interview unprepared, you should have a clear idea of what you hope to accomplish in your networking calls or meetings. It's also a good idea to let the other person know your objectives, so that you avoid wasted time and effort.

Build Relationship Equity

Your relationships in the workplace and marketplace are essential for business effectiveness, but don't stop there. Reach across industries. You build equity when the value of what you have appreciates. Invest in your relationships by making deposits of time, helping others, and staying in touch with peers, service people, former bosses, teachers, mentors, and advisors. The deposits may not always go to the person who made the investment. Meaning, you may make deposits with people who may not necessarily be able to reciprocate at that time. It's not always a direct exchange. You do want to establish a reputation as one who seeks to help and give to others. Over time, you will develop a reservoir of goodwill. When challenging times come—and they always do—you can tap into your relationship equity to make withdrawals by seeking advice, referrals for jobs, or support for your business.

NMC—Edie Fraser
Senior Consultant, Diversified Search
Advice for business owners and professionals looking to advance:

> Ask for counsel and think about what you can do for others. You can be excited about your products or services, but you need to know how to add value. Bring something special to the table. It needs to be a two-way street.
>
> Have a plan and set goals. Build an advisory board. Get the right advisors and listen to them. Assess the skill sets you need and go after them. Stay fervent on your growth plan.

Actively Chair Your Personal Board of Directors

Those who have been exposed to boards know that they require leadership. After all, the board chair or board president is at the helm of the organization. Part of the board's responsibility is to ensure that the organization and its resources are focused on its mission. First, if you have no directors, you need to cultivate relationships with experts who can provide you with valuable advice. Effective recruitment and leadership of a highly functioning board is essential and so is the ongoing management of those relationships. As you think through your board membership, be strategic. You want people who have held leadership positions and who bring unique talents in your circle. Look for chiefs: people who can bring expertise on key functional areas whether or not they have the official "C-Suite" titles—Chief Information Officer, Chief Human Resources Officer, Chief Financial Officer, Chief Legal Officer, etc. These people care about you enough to invest their time and resources to help you. Stay away from petty, jealous people who do not have your best interest at heart. You know who they are, so don't allow yourself to be seduced by their offers of help when in your heart you know they are working against you. Trust your gut.

Practice Your Message

There are those who achieve high office and significant career titles and are fair-to-average communicators. Whether you believe that there is a "black tax" (the notion that black people have to work and perform regular tasks twice as well as white people), you should strive for mastery relative to your communications. Regardless of your career stage, you must learn to articulate who you are and what you do. You must be able to promote your value to stay in the game.

Be of Service to Others

Women in general tend to fall into the "service mindset" particularly when it comes to family and community service. As it relates to networking, this can be an advantage. Think about how you can be helpful to others, whether it is sharing information, inviting others to an event that may be of value, assisting with a difficult task, or donating your time to a worthy cause. Doing for others will not only add value for them, but it will also build a reservoir of goodwill for you.

Make Technology Your Friend

The proliferation of new technologies is rapid. Just when you think you're up to speed with one tool, another one pops up. It's like the amusement park game of whack-a-mole where you constantly are trying to anticipate where the mole will pop up and get there in time to whack it. In this case, the "whack" is the adoption of new technology. Don't run from it. Use it selectively. See chapter six, "Winning with Social Media," for ways to turbo-charge your networking.

Execute Your Plan

It's never too early or too late to act on your networking plan. Be prepared for opportunities to leverage your skills and deploy the relevant aspects of your plan as needed.

NMC—Juliette C. Mayers
Executive Director, Multicultural Marketing Blue Cross Blue Shield of Massachusetts and Author
On how networking led to first career opportunity:

I started my professional career with GE Capital back in the eighties. During that time, Jack Welch was at the helm of GE, and the process for the Management Development Program was extensive and highly competitive. GE was the *crème de la crème* of leadership development, and a spot in the management program, with its on-the-job sink-or-swim management rotations in multiple states, was a highly desired trainee position. As a participant, my management rotations were in North Carolina, Ohio, and Connecticut. This experience provided a great launching pad for my career.

In retrospect, my selection into the program is a lesson in the power of networking.

During my senior year at Northeastern University in Boston, I attended a seminar with a speaker from GE; I was impressed. Immediately following the talk, I approached him, congratulated him on his presentation, and asked about opportunities at GE Capital. He informed me that they were not recruiting at Northeastern at that time. It was then that I eloquently delivered my elevator speech, letting him know that I was a marketing honor student who had completed internships at IBM, RJR

> Nabisco, and The Boston Globe; I worked three part-time jobs; was impressed with all of the wonderful things I heard about GE Capital and was interested in GE Capital's leadership development programs. I asked him to take my resume for consideration and he agreed. I requested a business card so that I could follow-up with him and I did. After two solid days of interviewing at GE Capital's headquarters in Stamford, Connecticut, I was hired into GE Capital's Management Development Program. The rest is history.

Preparation Matters

The outcome of my GE Capital example above would have been very different if I had been ill prepared, unknowledgeable about GE, and afraid to market myself. I also read the presenter well. The fact that the GE executive engaged students and was willing to talk after his presentation, signaled to me that this was someone who could be helpful. Clearly, his company had an interest at the university or he would not have accepted the speaking engagement and certainly would not have stayed around after his presentation.

From this chapter, we can draw some best practice tips for networking. Whether you are a seasoned professional, an entrepreneur or an up-and-coming associate, these universal tips apply:

- Have a plan. Review and modify your plan as necessary.

- Take time to reach out to others and sow the seeds to develop strong relationships.

- Make technology your friend.

- Be prepared to market your capabilities.

CHAPTER 6

Winning with Social Media

Winning with Social Media

Throughout black history, women have been the storytellers, social engineers, and catalysts for connecting families and communities. Today there are numerous social organizations and events within the black community serving as outlets for like-minded people. In churches, sororities, community organizations, and small entrepreneurial ventures, the success rate and number of women in leadership positions is high. However, this is not the case in the corporate world. The entertainment industry aside, it is certainly not true for large business ventures.

One of the beautiful things about the Internet is that it can provide a level playing field for those who invest the time to understand and use it wisely. With the proliferation of social media, there is an opportunity for black women to move beyond the offline social mastery to online business and economic empowerment. Additionally, social media can help to accelerate offline ventures and serve as a low-cost networking tool. Juliette Powell's book, *33 Million People in the Room*, provides insight into how President Barack Obama leveraged the Internet to supercharge his presidential campaign. Regardless of your political affiliation, President Barack Obama's use of social media serves as an example of how to effectively leverage these tools.

Social media lets people of all backgrounds and ethnicities into the conversation. It is a technological and networking revolution, as it shifts the balance of power from professional publishers and communicators, who often serve as "gatekeepers" of information, to individuals. In this new world, these tools allow access to those who take time to leverage the expansive opportunities. Without specialized training, small businesses can create a website, record videos, write and publish content, and much more. These powerful tools can accelerate brand building and ultimately fuel growth and effectiveness.

Let's start with how you can use social media to advance your career. Think of these tools as an extension of your brand. The same principles discussed in chapter two apply and can significantly accelerate and enhance the depth and breadth of your network. To get the most of these tools, you will need to develop and manage your brand and have a plan.

There are numerous social media venues; however, given our objective of advancing careers and growing businesses, only the most widely used (as of the writing of this book) are mentioned in the following pages. Regardless of the medium, you must do the work of defining your goals and objectives first. Once you do this, focus on the tools you need to help you execute your plan.

LinkedIn Facts (Source: LinkedIn.com)

- LinkedIn operates the world's largest professional network on the Internet with more than 100 million members in over 200 countries and territories.

- Roughly one million new members join LinkedIn every week. This is equivalent to one new member per second.

- More than half of LinkedIn members are currently located outside of the United States.

- There were nearly two billion people searches on LinkedIn in 2010.

- LinkedIn is currently available in six languages: English, French, German, Italian, Portuguese, and Spanish.

- As of January 2011, LinkedIn counts executives from all 2010 Fortune 500 companies as members; its hiring solutions were used by seventy-three of the Fortune 100 companies as of March 22, 2011.

- More than two million companies have LinkedIn Company Pages.

Tips for Using LinkedIn

Don't wait until you are looking for a job to use LinkedIn. Be proactive. Use this powerful tool to connect and stay in touch with others in your profession as well as cross-industry contacts. It's a great tool for your ICCs, HVCs, and MVCs, as well as new connections.

If you are in the job search mode, LinkedIn can accelerate your search. Here are tips for maximizing the power of LinkedIn:

- Complete your LinkedIn profile at (http://linkedin.com).

- Be sure to keep your profile updated. Use the "privacy settings" strategically. You can customize what, if anything, LinkedIn publishes about you when under the member profile section. Take the time to familiarize yourself with these options. To expand your knowledge, there is a little known "learning section" available on LinkedIn (http://learn.linkedin.com/). I also found *Sam's Teach Yourself LinkedIn* by Patrice-Anne Rutledge to be particularly helpful, as it is easy to read and follow.

- Join LinkedIn groups based on your area of interests. LinkedIn makes it easy to connect with affinity groups, and you also have the opportunity to create your own group and invite others to join.

Using LinkedIn to Find a Job

Personal branding guru Dan Schawbel, author of *Me 2.0*, has the following suggestions on finding a job using LinkedIn:

1. Establish your profile by copying the contents of your resume into the various LinkedIn fields.

2. Think about all of the keywords that a recruiter might use to find someone with your expertise, and then spread those keywords throughout your profile.

3. Edit your "public profile" to include a custom URL for your brand name, such as http://www.linkedin.com/in/danschawbel.

4. Your headline should position you for the career you want, not the job you have or had. It shouldn't read "Marketing Associate at XYZ Company." Instead, use keywords and a positioning statement, such as "SEO (search engine optimization expert) for small companies."

5. Get a recommendation from a previous job by giving a recommendation to one of your contacts first, without asking for anything in return.

6. Add three links to websites, blogs, or profiles that best represent your work professionally, using the full name of each website. For instance, use "Mark's Finance Blog" instead of just "blog."

7. Join LinkedIn groups, and start your own group based on your interests, either professionally or personal.

8. If you have a blog, add the Wordpress or Typepad application to your profile to highlight the last few posts you've written.

9. Import your contacts from your other social networks and e-mail database so that you have a foundation to build upon.

10. Search for specific jobs on LinkedIn, and try to locate people in your network who can forward introductions for you.

As LinkedIn is a professional network, Dan suggests you accept everyone as a new contact. By doing so, your second- and third-degree contacts will multiply as you build your first-degree contacts.

LinkedIn has numerous features. Some of them are as paid premium services for job hunting. Even without the paid features, you can use the following strategies to increase your visibility on LinkedIn.

LinkedIn Groups
Identify the affinity groups within your industry, and determine which ones are likely to be most useful. If you have an idea for a group that is not represented, start one and invite others to join the group. You can share information, ask questions, and identify opportunities to engage with others.

Leverage Links
Use the links on your profile to showcase relevant organizations such as your community work, professional services, or personal website.

Get the Word Out
If you are actively looking for a job, let your network know. If you are currently employed, you obviously don't want to put out an "all points bulletin" about your search. Here's where you may want to take advantage of LinkedIn's premium services to connect with recruiters, get notifications, and manage job opportunities.

Don't underestimate your friends. There are numerous stories of people who got leads from simply linking to others.

NMC—Cheryl Ginyard-Jones
Managing Principal – Energy & Utilities, Verizon Business
On networking and how LinkedIn led to her current role:

> Networking to me is actively connecting with people to give and get information, primarily to further business or professional aspirations, whether it's through professional organizations or through online tools like LinkedIn, Facebook, and Twitter. It can be in formal settings at conferences, business meetings, workshops or seminars, or informal settings such as coffee shops and restaurants. Believe it or not, one of my most active networking venues is my hair salon. I always encounter high-achieving, professional women. In this relaxed environment, women are often eager to engage in networking conversations. Stylists themselves are often great connectors since they serve clientele from a wide range of professional settings. My college alumni association is another great source of networking opportunities. These organizations are a great source of people who are in my field or related fields and are great for identifying professional opportunities, training, and resources.
>
> Networking has played a significant role in my career success. I can safely say that my last two jobs opportunities that I accepted were found through networking. One was through my graduate school alumni organization. My most recent job came as a result of linking to a friend of mine on LinkedIn.

Within an hour of linking with him, someone in his network sent me an inquiry regarding a role at his company. As a result, I am now employed with that company.

Networking has also played a big role in helping me find roles internally within a company. Just as in the external market, available jobs are not always posted on the jobs board. Even if they are, there are often candidates who are already short-listed for the role. I've reached out to the hiring manager well before a job is posted or early in the posting process; that has helped me get a leg up on my competition.

Facebook Facts (Source: Facebook.com)

About Facebook

Founded in February 2004, Facebook is a social utility that helps people communicate more efficiently with their friends, family, and coworkers. The company develops technologies that facilitate the sharing of information through the social graph, the digital mapping of people's real-world social connections. Anyone can sign up for Facebook and interact with the people they know in a trusted environment.

Users

With over 750 million active users (70 percent outside of the United States) and growing daily, 50 percent of active users log on to Facebook in any given day.

Product

Facebook, the product, is made up of core site functions and applications. Fundamental features to the experience on Facebook are a person's home page and profile. The home page includes the news feed, a personalized feed of his or her "friends'" updates. The profile displays information he or she has chosen to share, including interests, education, work background, and contact information. Facebook also includes core applications—photos, events, videos, groups, and pages —that let people connect and share in rich and engaging ways. Additionally, people can communicate with one another through chat, personal messages, wall posts, "pokes," or status updates.

Technology
Facebook is one of the most trafficked sites in the world and has had to build an infrastructure to support this rapid growth.

Platform
Facebook Platform is a development platform that enables companies and engineers to deeply integrate with the Facebook website and gain access to millions of users through the social graph. Facebook is a part of millions of people's lives all around the world providing unparalleled distribution potential for applications and the opportunity to build a business that is highly relevant to people's lives. More information can be found at http://developers.facebook.com.

Privacy, Safety and Security
Facebook has always focused on giving people control over their experience so they can express themselves freely while knowing that their information is being shared in the way they intend. Facebook's privacy policy is TRUSTe certified, and Facebook provides simple and powerful tools that allow people to control what information they share and with whom they share it. More information can be found at http://www.facebook.com/privacy/explanation.php. From its beginning, Facebook has worked to provide a safe and trusted environment by requiring that people use their real names, for

example. Facebook also works with online safety experts around the world and has established a global Safety Advisory Board that it consults with on safety issues. More information can be found at http://www.facebook.com/fbsafety and http://www.facebook.com/security.

Using Facebook to Advance Your Business

You are probably familiar with Facebook's profile pages, but did you know that Facebook also has business pages? You can post videos, events, updates, photos, and other applications. Set up your Facebook page at www.Facebook.com/pages, and click the "create a page" button. It's that simple.

Social media branding is equally as important as offline branding. Dan Schawbel, personal branding guru and author of *ME 2.0,* has these five tips for social networking sites:

1) **Discover your brand before you communicate it.** You need to identify what you want to stand for: your mission values, brand attributes, and how you're differentiated in your industry. It's hard to reflect on what your strengths and long-term goals are, but without identifying them, you will end up rebranding yourself many times without a sense of purpose.

2) **Protect your brand by reserving your full name everywhere.** You need to own your digital property before someone else does. This includes your domain name (yourname.com) and your full name on social networks such as Facebook, Twitter, YouTube, and others that are relevant to your brand. For example, if you're a real estate agent, you should join Active Rain (www.activerain.com). Also, you can have more control over the Google search results for your name because all these networks rank high in Google.

3) **Set up a system where you can manage your on-line reputation.** To keep a pulse on your brand, you should set up a comprehensive Google alert (Google. com/alerts) for your name. This way, anytime your name is mentioned in a blog post or news article, you're aware of it. You should also use Facebook search and BoardTracker.com for discussion forum mentions. If you neglect observing and responding to brand mentions, you risk negative word of mouth, which can travel very fast online.

4) **Choose a single picture, name, motto, and theme—and use it consistently.** As with a corporate brand, consistency is key, which means you should have the same presence everywhere online and offline. Take one professional headshot of yourself and use it as your avatar on social networks, on your blog or website, on your business cards, and other places where your name is mentioned. If your name is Matthew but you want to be called Matt, then use that name everywhere and don't change it. You can have a motto or tagline just like Nike or another brand as long as you use it repeatedly. The same goes with your overall theme, including font, color, and style.

5) **Publish content so people get a sense of your voice, not just your resume.** A resume isn't a differentiator anymore. Now you need an active voice online by publishing content. When you publish, it helps you to become more visible and credible and to connect with more people. Innovative companies want people with fresh ideas and different thinking, which is why participating in online forums is so important these days.

NMC—Colette A.M. Phillips
President and CEO, Colette Phillips Communications and
Founder of Get Konnected
Perspective on online and offline networking:

Online networking seems to be growing. There
is a bigger distinction in traditional versus non-
traditional networking among older versus younger
professionals. Older people put more stock in offline networking. While there is increased adoption
of online networking, most decisions are still made
through offline networking. If there isn't a personal
connection, online networking will be treated with
a healthy dose of skepticism. You need a blend of the
two—both offline and online. Network regionally
and nationally. Make the investment in yourself.

NMC—Kathy Taylor
Associate Vice President, Community Development at Road
Scholar
On offline balance:

Black women need to attend at least one networking conference annually—an event designed to enhance our professional, personal, and financial fu-
tures. You will also gain an understanding of issues
and trends facing black women. Take the opportunity to enjoy restorative activities that are spiritual, physical, and mental. It takes a tremendous
amount of energy and time to maintain your focus
on being successful and/or leading effective teams.
It is vital to your well-being and future success to
find and apply balance.

Networking Etiquette

Networking Etiquette

I've learned that people will forget what you said, people will forget what you did, but people will never forget how you made them feel.

—Maya Angelou

In today's time-pressured, digital world, face-to-face communication remains a highly valued interaction. Treasure those moments to connect "live" whenever possible and familiarize yourself with the professional courtesies. Fortunately, there are numerous books on the topic on the soup-to-nuts of general etiquette. That is not the intent of this chapter. Here I will focus on some of the essentials for enhancing your networking effectiveness. I've developed an approach for networking engagement that is applicable for any relationship. I've dubbed this approach "HEARTS."

In addition, I will cover some of the basics for business etiquette that professionals sometimes forget. These are intended to enhance your brand and your effectiveness.

HEARTS—Networking Essentials

H—Honesty and integrity will help you build trusting productive relationships. Your actions should be consistent with your words. People will pay close attention to what you do, not just what you say. Be transparent in your dealings, and do what you say you're going to do! Bring your authentic self to every interaction. If you don't, you will pay a tremendous price on your health, finances, and relationships.

E—Energy and enthusiasm are infectious twin attributes that you must exude. People want to associate with others who exhibit positive energy and are passionate about their work and their product(s). Show conviction in all aspects of your work, your communications, and your physical presence. While we're on "E," let's not forget exercise. It does wonders for your mind, body and energy level.

A—Attitude! Having a positive attitude and operating from a place of abundance accelerates growth. Abundant thinkers realize that there is enough for everyone and that by helping others and giving selflessly, more opportunities are created, not fewer. Give liberally and with a positive attitude.

R—"R-E-S-P-E-C-T. *Find out what it means to me.*" Thank you, Aretha Franklin, for calling attention to this important word. Respect is something that *everyone* wants, and this is true across all cultures. Demonstrate respect through your actions by valuing differences, adopting an inclusive approach, valuing the unique contributions of others, and communicating in culturally competent ways.

T—"Thanks" is a powerful six-letter word that cannot be overused. Be appreciative of the things that others do for you. Don't take them for granted. Never be too busy to say thank you. A simple handwritten card can differentiate you from the crowd and bring a smile to the receiver of your kind gesture.

S—Smile. Practice smiling and make it part of your toolkit when you approach others and when you're on the phone. Unless the occasion is a sad one, this simple gesture makes you more approachable. It doesn't mean you have to grin from ear to ear. It's more about your approach, and smiling tends to thaw the ice. Try it!

Navigating the Networking Lunch

It is perfectly okay to extend lunch (or other meal), invitations to people you are seeking to get to know better and with whom you have already established a relationship. E-mail is an acceptable method for a lunch invitation. It is generally a good idea to include multiple options for dates once your guest(s) have agreed to this method of connecting with you. Be clear about the purpose of the lunch. This will help to set the expectations for your meeting.

Punctuality is a must. Say no to "CP (colored people's) time." For some this is a cultural stereotype that refers to people who are always late and for others it is a mode of operation. Ladies, there is absolutely no place for being late. Punctuality is not only expected, but it is a reflection of your level of professionalism and respect for the other person's time. Plan your day and travels accordingly so that you will arrive at the designated place at least five minutes ahead of schedule. In case of an emergency that causes you to be late, call ahead to the restaurant and give your guests the courtesy of a message.

Prepare to have a conversation. Give some advance thought and planning for your networking connection. You don't need a script, but you should have a goal of what you hope to accomplish for the lunch meeting and key things you want to discuss.

As the one extending the invitation, you are expected to pay for the meal. Let your guest know that the lunch is your treat. You can articulate this verbally or immediately take the luncheon check when it arrives. Certainly, if your guest insists on paying for lunch or offers to go Dutch, it is okay to accept, particularly if the person is a senior executive.

Lunch Table Tips (Selected Tips for the Business Luncheon)

1. Choose a lunch location that is convenient for your guest.

2. Request a telephone number that is frequently checked by your guest—ideally, a business cell phone number. Provide your mobile contact information as well.

3. Once you arrive at the luncheon destination, put away your cell phone and any items that can cause distraction.

4. Give your guest a warm welcome and the best seating.

5. Place your napkin in your lap immediately after you are seated.

6. Allow your guest to order first.

7. Order foods that are easy to handle and that are less likely to end up on your clothing or between your teeth.

8. Use the appropriate utensils for your meals. When in doubt, use the utensils from the outside in.

9. Thank your wait staff and your guest(s).

10. Follow up your lunch meeting with a written communiqué. Yes, e-mail is fine, but a handwritten card is better, as it will make you stand out.

Returning Telephone Calls

Your network is broader than people you meet at business events; it also includes those in your day-to-day business dealings. When a work colleague calls, return the call as soon as possible, but do not exceed forty-eight hours. Not returning the call of a colleague is disrespectful and rude, yet there seems to be more acceptance of this unprofessional practice. Do not perpetuate this bad habit. It damages your brand and could later come back to haunt you.

If you are completely swamped and the request can't be fulfilled immediately, at least acknowledge the contact and let the person know that you plan to follow up with her later when your schedule eases.

Handling Other Networking Calls

Should you return telephone calls for those wishing to network with you? It depends. For those with whom you have an established connection, make a point of returning calls within forty-eight hours of contact. If you cannot meet this timeframe, don't fret, but do acknowledge the call by either having your assistant get back to the person or call during off-peak hours.

If the call is specific and you can take action, do so rather than procrastinate. For example, you met a senior executive who spoke at a conference you attended a few months ago. The person was very impressed by your presentation and called to invite you to present your topic at a business forum she is hosting. In this instance, if you have enough information to make an assessment, you can check your schedule, determine whether the opportunity makes sense for you, hold the time open, and schedule a specific time to speak with the caller.

In another instance, you have received three calls from a hotshot entrepreneur you met at an event where you spoke about the importance of networking. She is looking to meet with your marketing director and would like you to set up a meeting for her to do so. This is her third call to you within two business days. You did not give her your business card, but you do remember her. Should you return the call? You are not obligated to do so, but it is up to you. You could let her know that your firm is already working with a vendor who offers the same services and is not in the market to make a change. Your assistant can place the call to her and acknowledge receipt of the message letting her know that you will call at a later date, or you may choose to make time to have a brief conversation with her.

Realistically, busy professionals cannot give equal weight to everyone who wishes to network with them. You have to be selective. In so doing, consider your networking tiers (ICC, HVC and MVC) and align activities with your goals. Above all, be respectful in your communications even when you say "No."

When attending networking forums, schedule an hour within the two days following the session to return calls and to follow-up on key connections that you want to cultivate.

If you are following up on a discussion or commitment, it is okay to send more than one e-mail or telephone call to the person as long as you are respectful. Often professionals and entrepreneurs, though well-intentioned, are overwhelmed with e-mails and telephone calls. Be specific in your communications and always be polite. When leaving a voice message, say your name, state your objective, and clearly provide the number where you can be reached. Repeat the number for your listener's convenience. It is annoying and inefficient to have to replay a message multiple times to try to decipher the person's name and/or telephone number. By leaving a detailed, succinct message, the receiver of your message will have enough information to take action. Unless your topic is highly sensitive and confidential, don't leave them guessing regarding your call.

Social and Professional Networking Invitations

Should you accept invitations from social networking and professional networking websites? Again, it depends. Be careful who you befriend and invite into your personal network. I recommend reserving personal networks such as Facebook (not Facebook Pages) for friends and family. Do not accept invitations from those wishing to befriend you in this way if the person is not a personal friend. For professional networks, it is not as clear-cut. For professional invitations such as those on LinkedIn, you should determine your objective and your plans for using the tool, and let that be your guide. If you are looking to build the largest set of professional connections possible, then you should accept all requests. On the other hand, if you are looking to use the tool selectively for endorsements and referrals of trusted sources with whom you have close connection (e.g. your HVCs), then you should accept invitations only from those for whom you have a professional working knowledge.

A Word about Invitations to Paid Events

Most of us like to be invited to swanky events. It's great to be included, isn't it?

If you are inviting someone to a paid event, please be honest and upfront about it. Do not use the word "guest" as in "please come as my guest," unless you plan to pick up the tab or provide complimentary tickets. On a number of occasions, I've received such an invitation. After accepting, I got a second message letting me know that the cost of the event was $250 and I needed to forward a check for that amount to the individual. In one instance, I paid the fee; however, I felt bamboozled. I was not amused by the sly approach that they used. This method of operating is a major violation of the first of the HEARTS approach: honesty. Be upfront about invitations that require an outlay of cash. What do you think I did when I received the next invitation from that individual asking me to come as their guest? Nuff said.

Company Dinners or Community Galas

You may work for a large organization, purchased a ticket to support a community event, or perhaps you are a guest of an organization hosting a dinner. Regardless of how you got there, these events are great opportunities for networking. While it is an opportunity to see some people you may know, make a point of connecting with at least two people you do not know. Always introduce yourself to the other guests or colleagues at the table. If you are the table host, be sure to greet each person at your table even if you already know them.

Referrals

If you know the person well and can personally vouch for them, by all means, do so. When you do refer someone, whenever possible, make a warm in-person introduction. Depending on the nature of the referral, you can schedule breakfast or lunch with the parties. This works well for important referrals that can likely lead to significant business opportunities or win/win alliances. If this is not feasible, provide some context for the referral. You can do this by e-mail or by voicemail.

Be considerate of other people's time when referring others. In today's hectic business environment, time is very precious. Before referring others, be thoughtful and use those requests judiciously.

Job References

For professional-level jobs, many times recruiters will leverage their network to find out about candidates. Likewise, job seekers will reach out to their network to find out about a company, hiring executive, or the opportunity. When using someone as a reference, make sure you let the person know in advance and obtain her permission. Sometimes those who have been in the workforce for an extended length of time forget these career basics. You should always arm your reference with a recent copy of your resume, a description of the job for which you are being considered, and key points that you think are relevant to communicate.

Business Card Exchange

Your business card is a marketing and networking tool. Make sure that it is high quality and professionally designed. Use a business card case to ensure easy access to your cards and to protect them from discoloration, stains, and the like. In keeping with our strategic networking approach, distribute your card selectively. Once you have established a common interest and a reason and have mutual agreement to contact the other person with whom you are networking, you can use the following tips:

- When giving your business card, hold the card at the corner with the information facing towards the other person.

- When receiving someone else's card, take a second to look at the card and thank them.

- Use the back of the card to jot a note to yourself about the person or any action items relevant to your discussion. You may also want to include a note on the back of the card to help you remember the person, e.g. "Simmons Grad., red suit, knows Pam." I find this to be particularly useful at large events where you may end the evening with five or more cards.

- After the meeting or event, follow up on any action items that you have noted on the card and transfer the card to your contact system. While you're at it, you should send a LinkedIn request while the information is fresh on your mind.

Nametags
Wear your nametag on your right hand side. When shaking hands, it's a lot easier to glance at the nametag. If you are hosting the event, be sure to place both the first name and last name on the nametag and use a large easy-to-read font.

Make Them the Center of Your Universe
You're at a reception having a wonderful time getting to know Sue. There's only one annoying problem: Sue keeps glancing around the room. The minute she sees Joe, she abruptly ends the conversation and greets him. There are legitimate reasons why this could happen. It is possible that Sue invited Joe and wants to make sure he is welcomed appropriately; however, you are feeling dumped by Sue, right? Managing transitions can be tricky. In this instance, the appropriate thing for Sue to do is to give you a heads-up.

"Jenny, just so you know, I'm not being rude, I am expecting my colleague Joe to arrive any minute. He's on a tight schedule, so once he arrives, I need to introduce him to Jan, so forgive me if it seems that I'm glancing towards the door." Better still, Sue should wait for Joe near the entrance to avoid this scenario all together. Make your networking colleague the center of attention.

Handling RSVPs

Give your requester the courtesy of a response. RSVP, used on most invitations, is a French term *Respondez s'il vous plait.* It means "respond if you please," or simply, "please respond." Whether your invitation is in writing or an electronic communiqué such as Evite and e-mail, you should let your requester know your intentions. It is a common courtesy, allowing your host to plan accordingly. This is true not just for formal events but for meetings as well.

Etiquette and Your Brand

How you interact with people and the attributes that you exhibit in doing so, make a marked difference in how you are perceived and positively impacts the lives of others. Commit your self to embracing the HEARTS networking essentials and to practicing good business etiquette.

CHAPTER 8
"The Only One"

CHAPTER 8

"The Only One"

You must be willing to take a risk; without risk-taking,
you will not go far.

—Elvoid Mayers

The time has come to end the isolation that is so prevalent for
many people of color. Whether you're in a formal organization
or in an entrepreneurial venture, too often the proverbial village
that is required for fostering inclusion and sustaining successful
engagement is nonexistent.

Earlier in my career, I started the first African American
Resource Group (AARG) at a very large multinational financial
institution in Boston, Massachusetts. At the time I was a marketing manager in a large department, but I was still experiencing
personal isolation. As a black woman, the experience was not
new; however, at that point, I was dealing with one of the most
painful experiences in my life—the loss of my unborn child after
the four-month "safety mark." Most miscarriages occur within a
three-month window, so once I had passed that hurdle, I shared the
news of my pregnancy. For what seemed like an eternity, I relived
the anguish each time a well-meaning colleague congratulated
me on the pregnancy.

With every explanation, the experience remained vivid. Eventually, after what seemed like an eternity, the comments stopped. This was a defining moment in my life, as it caused me to think deeply about my work relationships, personal relationships, and my career. I dealt with my personal pain by praying, and I threw myself into work.

I eventually reached out to colleagues and sought out other African Americans throughout the company. From that experience, I emerged fearless and determined to end the isolation I experienced in the workplace. It was helpful to have a wonderful, supportive boss at the time. With his blessing and the help of a few brave friends, a new path was created.

After reaching out across the large company, the resource group's membership blossomed to over two hundred employees. The majority of the black employees were in departments where they happened to be the only person of color. Within a two-year period, the constructive engagement of the employees who participated in the group got the attention of the CEO.

Together the associates identified key issues that hampered the black employees' ability to bring their "true selves" to the workplace. They participated in development activities, worked with human resources to address advancement barriers, and established ongoing communication with executive leadership. Before long, black employees had a voice, a budget, and the support of leadership in tackling some of the structural changes required to address key issues. Another defining moment was the implementation of the first-ever "Diversity in Action" companywide forum, which was organized by AARG and chaired by the CEO. Leading AARG came with its own set of challenges, but the experience reinforced the idea that change occurs when we work together, take risks, and engage constructively.

Prior to achieving critical mass and organizing an agenda, the individual voices of black employees were just that—individual voices. Their efforts, while similar, were uncoordinated, fragmented, and dispersed. In their article, "Power and Influence in Organizations," Joanne Martin and Debra Meyerson describe this type of action as "disorganized co-action (Martin and Meyerson 1998)." It is incredibly difficult to drive change, achieve inclusion, and most important, maximize effectiveness in business and in life without a focused strategy and true connection with others who can identify with and support your agenda.

Through AARG and the support of leaders who listened, the organization redefined its approach to diversity and inclusion. As a result, other employee groups were formed. Don't underestimate your ability to influence change.

An Alternative Path Forward

How many times have you been in room and looked around, and discovered you were the *only* one of color? How did it make you feel? If this is still your reality, how does it make you feel? In this age of job insecurity and high unemployment, many workers are reluctant to address issues that are affecting them. So what can you as an individual do? Here are some practical tips:

- **Be positive.** It is a state of being that has tremendous impact on your mind, body, and soul. Each interaction with an associate, friend, or work colleague is a reflection of your personal brand. You wouldn't spend your hard-earned money on a product that evoked negativity for you. Don't spend your human capital with negative people. This is a very crucial point. Each interaction matters; whenever possible, make it a positive one.

- **Assume positive intent.** Approach each situation and interaction with the expectation that it will be positive. Cut yourself, your colleagues, and your business associates, some slack. With the exception of a small minority, most people are well-intentioned. Approach with a smile. It's a very powerful tool and it's great for your health!

- **Have an attitude of gratitude.** Give thanks for all that you are and all that you have. The fact that you are reading this book tells me that you are privileged and have a lot for which to be thankful. Focus on all of the positive things in your life. That which gets your positive energy and your focus will grow stronger and better—relationships included.

- **Exercise your body and your mind.** What does exercise have to do with networking or relationships? A lot. When you exercise, you feed your body, your spirit, and your mind. The release of all of those healthy endorphins adds to your wellbeing. It is equally important to consistently and systematically read and engage in activities that require you to learn new things. It makes for a healthier and a more interesting you!

- **Support your fellow sisters.** You've probably heard of the "crabs in a barrel" concept where the crabs have difficulty getting out of the barrel because they keep pulling the ones in front of them down. Too often this dynamic plays out in the workplace and marketplace.

  Think of the business pie as infinite. Find ways to support other women whether it's through sharing information, purchasing products or services, or advocating for a colleague who is not in the room. These types of affirmative actions will propel you and others forward.

- **Secure your financial future.** Practice good financial stewardship. It is a mindset. It's not about how much money you make but about how much you keep. In order to accumulate wealth, you must master basic habits such as budgeting, automatic saving, and living within your means.

  I am amazed at the number of high-income women who are living from paycheck to paycheck. Stop the madness now! Commit to restructuring your finances to accumulate appreciable assets and savings that you can pass on to your heirs or fall back on in the event of a crisis. There are many free online resources to get you started. Use them.

- **Don't be a victim. Be a victor!** As an individual, you have the power to influence positive changes even when you are the only one. Use your networking skills to build relationships across cultures. Step outside your comfort zone to create relationships with people who will support you and help you reach your objectives.

Black women are skilled leaders in many social organizations, whether it's church, a sorority or some other community center. Too many hiring managers use the excuse, "We can't find them," when it comes to selecting qualified black women. To address those isolation and scarcity issues, the talents used in social organizations must be parlayed into the business and professional environments.

It is imperative that we embrace the role of teacher, bridge-builder, advocate, and change agent. This is a huge risk depending on your situation, but it is a bigger risk not to take the lead. It doesn't seem fair, does it? Why must blacks play roles that will help others feel comfortable? When will we arrive at a place where people are inclusive in their thinking and truly value the contributions of black women? These are all great questions. Black women in significant corporate roles are still a novelty. Perhaps when a critical mass is reached, these issues will subside; however, we have not yet reached that milestone.

Look for partners in the struggle. When I reflect on key defining moments in my life, those moments where I took significant risks and acted with conviction, I realized they tended to follow significant challenges. Such was the case when I founded the AARG—and history has shown this pattern to be true.

In order to end the isolation, you must identify others who (regardless of race or gender) have an interest in creating and advancing a shared agenda. One of my most exciting roles was leading the Ad Club Foundation in the mid-90s. The organization was committed to advancing diversity in the communications industry and was founded by the Advertising Club of Greater Boston (the Ad Club). At that time, Elizabeth Cook was at the helm of the Ad Club. I could write a book about my tenure at the Ad Club Foundation, but for our purposes, I'd like to focus on a leader who exemplified sincere efforts to build cultural bridges.

NMC—Elizabeth Cook
Former President, Ad Club of Greater Boston

Through her leadership, Elizabeth Cook paved the way for many women and people of color, including me. She is a pioneer and as such, has a long list of firsts—to name a few:

- First class of MBAs at Simmons Graduate School of Management

- First among a small group of visionary women to form The Boston Club

- President of the Advertising Club of Greater Boston, the largest advertising industry association in the country at the time

- Established the Ad Club Foundation to address racial and ethnic diversity in the communications industry

- Mentor and advisor to many women who have gone on to prominence

Elizabeth's perspective on networking, gender and the glass ceiling:

As a divorced single mom, I did not have a clear path. I had to figure out how to make a living, and I did not have the benefit of mentors. Networking helped me to find solutions to the challenges that I had. For example: I was accepted into Harvard Business School, but decided not to go given the economics at that time. There were few options for women supporting themselves back then. Through networking, I learned that two women from Harvard were starting a school for women, the Simmons Graduate School of Management.

I think women have more empathy for sure. As a single mom, I would empathize with other single moms who were trying to advance in the workplace. I also empathize with women of color because I know they have a harder road to hoe. In the main, women are empathetic and this influences how they reach out to help others.

Sexism is still out there. It's in cocktail party jokes, etc. Some men are still struggling with equality. It all depends. Some women have managed to get to the top. Women are still struggling with diversity as it relates to race and gender at the top of the house. Women need to pay attention to the culture of the organization and make choices based on that. At the board level, women directors need to speak up and make their voices heard.

Help Organizations Address Barriers

In their book *Breaking Through: The Making of Minority Executives in Corporate America*, David A. Thomas and John J. Gabarro explore pathways to success for minorities. The authors assert that breakthroughs can happen if individuals and organizations understand the roles that they play in creating the opportunities that enable minority executives to reach the top. We'll revisit this in the next chapter, "Play to Win."

Find a Mentor

Everyone can benefit from mentoring. Having a mentor requires a measure of humility, the ability to accept candid feedback, and the will to take the necessary actions to ensure continuous improvement. The mentors who are in my life today are the ones with whom I had a personal connection or shared agenda. My mentors span the gamut—from peers in different industries, CEOs I've worked with in a community leadership capacity or through board service, and my dear friend Martha.

Interesting, my staunchest advocates and mentors have been from a variety of racial and ethnic backgrounds and some of these people are included in this book. In this instance, I am talking about mentoring relationships that by definition require a high degree of trust. This is someone who has your back, truly cares about your development, and will tell you the truth without judgment. This is the type of relationship that will accelerate your growth and your opportunities.

Stacy Blake-Beard, Ph.D., is a well-known expert on mentoring and sheds light on this important topic.

NMC—Stacy Blake-Beard, Ph.D.
On finding a mentor:

Mentoring relationships provide an excellent forum to hone and develop Goleman's five dimensions of emotional intelligence—self-awareness, self-regulation, empathy, social skills, and understanding what motivates you and others.

Trust is an important aspect. Mentoring requires a level of vulnerability and willingness to open yourself up. It is special and different from other developmental relationships. To gain the most from mentoring, there has to be a willingness to be vulnerable. Often our protective defensiveness gets in the way of good mentoring. We have to be willing to hear critical feedback. We also need to make the time to solicit feedback. We have to make it a priority.

There is no one perfect right way to develop effective mentoring partnerships. But there are some tried-and-true practices that can stimulate the development of these important relationships. Survey the landscape and figure out who can help you and how. There should be reciprocity, mutual learning, and growth in an effective mentoring relationship. Think about what you bring to the table. Use your networking skills to get on your prospective mentor's calendar. Once you do, be judicious with her time. Here's how to groom a mentor:

- Do your own self-assessment. Where do you want to go? What are your goals? What are your strengths and your developmental needs?

- Survey the landscape. Figure out who is out there. Talk to people who are connected to your prospective mentor.

- Get on your prospective mentor's calendar.

- Go to that first meeting with an agenda.

- Ask questions. With the right invitation, people enjoy sharing their experiences and perspective with others.

- Follow up the meeting with a handwritten note.

- Make "the ask" for a second meeting.

- Do what you say you are going to do.

Mentoring *Plus* The Role of Sponsors

Stacy's advice is action-oriented and requires you to take the initiative in the mentoring relationship. In addition to mentoring, seek out professional development opportunities with organizations with specific programming for black professionals. The nuances do matter, and you need strategies and support from those who get it. As I mentioned in the beginning of this book, the Executive Leadership Council's (ELC) Pipeline Leadership Program was a wonderful gift, and I will forever treasure the relationships I have with my Pipeline Sisters. I also realize that participation in this program is a privilege that is not accessible to all, so seek out the programs in your respective market that may work for you.

The Partnership Inc. is another organization with a number of well-designed programs specifically tailored for people of color. Dr. Beverly Edgehill, CEO of The Partnership Inc., shares her perspective on mentoring:

NMC—Dr. Beverly Edgehill
CEO, The Partnership Inc.
On mentoring and sponsorship:

In general, mentoring is critical. I couldn't have gotten to this point without having many mentors along the way. Mentors walk with you along the path. They are your guides. I'm a big supporter of mentors because you can't travel the career journey alone. In terms of effectiveness, you need a mentor who will tell you the truth about yourself. It is imperative that you see feedback as a gift. Some people can't handle feedback, and it hinders their ability to progress to the next assignment.

In addition to mentors, you need sponsors. The sponsor is the one who opens the door for the opportunity and will stand behind you. These are two different roles. If you're in the early stages of your career, you can move forward without a sponsor. When you get to a certain stage of contribution, you must have a sponsor to move your career forward.

You need people in your network to help you look at your career objectively throughout your working life. Some of the skills that worked earlier in your career can be a detriment later on. For example, the "I have to be strong; I can't let anybody see me weak," mindset works against you. There are times when you need to be seen as vulnerable and as someone who asks for help. This is part of being emotionally aware and mature. Leaders who have a greater degree of emotional intelligence tend to have a greater impact.

Tracy Gray-Walker has experienced mentoring from all aspects—as a mentor, mentee, and peer mentor. In addition to her day job, Tracey is a member of the Executive Leadership Council.

NMC—Tracey Gray-Walker
Senior Vice President and Chief Diversity Officer, AXA Equitable
Perspective on mentoring and sponsorship:

> Mentoring is very important, but so is sponsorship. I'll start with mentoring. The basic requirements of an effective mentoring relationship are honesty, trust, compassion, and willingness to share. Mentors must be willing to go outside of their normal operating model and help others with the knowledge they have. Mentees should ask for help, be open to feedback, and be committed to following through on their commitments.
>
> I also think that it's important to have multiple mentors. Putting together a comprehensive strategy for success requires help from multiple places.
>
> In terms of relationship management, mentees need to own the relationship, nurture it, schedule the appointments, and proactively think about what they need from the mentor in terms of development.
>
> I mentioned the importance of sponsorship. While you don't necessarily pick a sponsor, you must be willing to build relationships with key people in the organization. They should understand where you want to go. With sponsors, you want to position yourself in a positive light. They need to see all your successes.

Keep Hope Alive

I am blessed to have my mother-in-law, Elvoid Mayers (Ellie), in my life and smart enough to heed her sage advice. When I discussed the concept for this book with her, she suggested the inclusion of this chapter, "The Only One."

NMC—Elvoid Mayers
Retired Educator, Chair of Social Studies Department, Rockland Public Schools
On being "the only one" and taking risks:

I went to an all-black college—Livingstone College in Salisbury, NC. It was the only college at the time that was established by blacks and funded by blacks.

I was an educator for forty-two years and was the first African American state president of Alpha Epsilon of Delta Kappa Gamma Society International (an organization dedicated to the advancement of women in education) for the state of Massachusetts.

Networking was a significant factor in my career advancement. I didn't look for it, but it was something others saw in me and they pointed me in the right direction. Someone is always watching you to see how you react to different situations. You have to take action. This, together with mentoring, helped me to move forward.

In the field of education, most teachers were women. However, it was mostly men at the leadership level. There were no female superintendents in Massachusetts until the 1960s. Until joining the society of Delta Kappa Gamma Society International, I was not aware of organized networking opportunities for women.

It's difficult for black women to talk about the glass ceiling because it's more like the concrete ceiling, particularly if you're the only one or one of a few. You really have to align yourself with your white colleagues and have them bring you along. Very often, blacks in positions of power are reluctant to take risks with other blacks because they are the only ones, and this perpetuates the glass ceiling dynamic. Black women must also work with each other and support each other in order to crack the glass ceiling.

Depending on your field, there may be a push for diversity. Certain positions are not viewed as ones that black people can hold. Often times white women do not want to work for women of color. People have mental limits on what positions you can be in; there is an attitude that you have to "stay in your place" and work within the confines of your situation. If people don't reach out to you, reach out to them. Keep your eyes on your goal. You have to assert yourself without being brash or turning people off. Don't allow others to overlook you. You have to advocate for yourself.

Often, the people who can influence your career are of a different race. You have to work within the framework that you have. It is important to build cross-cultural relationships. You need a mentor, and you have to be in tune with your mentor. When there was an opportunity for a job as department head, my mentor (a white male) suggested that I apply for the position and hand-deliver it to the hiring manager's office. I got the job, and the rest is history.

> You have to be willing to take risks. Don't just think about what you can lose but what you can gain. It is important to reach out and keep your eyes on your goals.
>
> Don't be intimidated by being the "only one." You need to get comfortable with being around people of all races and cultures.

Peer Mentoring

Self-advocacy, mentoring, and sponsorship are essential to moving forward. By now, it should be clear that having a "lone wolf" status is not a good thing. In addition to the brilliant concepts shared by our NMCs on this topic, don't overlook the power of peer mentoring. One of the gifts of the ELC Pipeline Sisters connection is the ongoing source of support from these women. Identify peers you respect and trust. Share your stories, strategize on ways that you can help and support each other. Add this additional source to your toolkit. It is also a great way to expand the network, so reach out within and outside of your industry.

Rewrite The Script

I love to write. I have found it to be a very powerful means of expression. In life, each one of us has a script. Like writers, we have an opportunity to strengthen our future stories, through reflection.

We cannot change the past, but we do have tremendous opportunity to shape the future. Through personal sharing, mentoring and active management of our networks and a commitment to drive change within our environments, we can create new experiences. Start now! Take a few minutes to reflect on this chapter and write the answers to the following questions:

What aspects of "The Only One" resonated with you?

What specific action(s) will you take to address isolation (on-going or incidental)?

What will you do to support other women?

Share your story. Identify at least two people with whom you plan to share your story.

CHAPTER 9

Play to Win

CHAPTER 9

Play to Win

The time for the healing of the wounds has come. The
moment to bridge the chasms that divide us has come.
The time to build is upon us.

—Nelson Mandela

My purpose in writing this chapter is to bring focus to some
of the issues that affect the advancement of black women—
gender issues, racial dynamics, and lack of access to well-placed
mentors and sponsors. Equally important is the examination of
solutions and conversations that will increase understanding and
ultimately lead to positive outcomes.

As I reviewed the first draft of the chapter, I reflected on
Mandela's quote: *The time for the healing of the wounds has come. The
moment to bridge the chasms that divide us has come. The time to build is
upon us.* While by no means do the issues I referenced rise to the
level of Mandela's challenge with apartheid, I do find inspiration
in his actions, skill at diplomacy, mastery in finding common
ground, and in his incredible patience in addressing an extremely
critical issue.

The Slippery Slopes of Race and Gender

As it relates to networking, what if you've done everything that you are supposed to do, and you can't seem to move the needle when it comes to advancing your business? You've reached out and have networked within your organization and across industries, and you have the right products and services. You have the credentials. You've produced impressive business results, and you watch as your white counterparts advance. What's up with that? Is it racism, sexism, or is it something else? Could it be both? How does one really know? And even if you know, does it really make a difference? Regardless of the intent, isn't the impact the same?

In *Our Separate Ways*, Bell and Nkomo describe the "bicultural" nature of the African American woman's experience. For African American women, biculturality (or moving from one cultural context to another) requires that black women shape their careers in the white world, while shaping other dimensions of their lives in the black community. Bicultural stress is a psychological barrier black professional women feel when they are compelled to suppress or diminish one part of their identity in order to exist in either of the cultural contexts where they work or live (Bell and Nkomo 2001). *Heavy stuff.*

While it is often difficult to tell how much of a role race plays, it remains a major factor in the consciousness of our society. Sadly, real or perceived racism is not only taking a psychological toll, but a physical one as well. Research shows that racism contributes to significant social and health disparities in many communities. As Dr. Derald Wing Sue points out in his book *Micro Aggressions in Everyday Life: Race, Gender, and Sexual Orientation,* blacks are still faced with micro-aggressions and micro-assaults daily that lead to sustained and dangerous levels of stress.

With the election of President Barack Obama in 2008, some conversations quickly turned to discussion of a post-racial society. To summarize, support for the post-racial society might say something to this effect: "The fact that a biracial man was elected to the highest office in the land means that our work is done, and all racial minorities now have access to opportunities and fair treatment." No disrespect to those who genuinely believe that such a time has arrived, but the realities of racial minorities do not support it. Structural and institutional racism were hundreds of years in the making and will take many years to eradicate.

Slights, real or perceived, remain in the consciousness of many people of color. It is important to acknowledge the undercurrents and issues affecting relationships in the work and marketplace. It is essential that black women focus on health and take actions to mitigate the potential impact of well-documented forces with the potential to derail your dream and your health. While caring for the emotional and physical health is important, spiritual health is an important foundation and completes the picture for excellent overall health. You must continue to move forward. Stay focused on your goals and work constructively to create opportunities for yourself and others. Keep moving.

The Role of Politics

Broadly speaking, politics refers to a process by which groups of people make decisions and govern. Whether formally or informally, people in positions of power tend to set the tone and apply the rules for the organization. I have yet to work for an organization where the rules for decision-making and governance are written down. Even if they were, there are always unspoken ones and ways of operating that come only through observation and analysis of behaviors. Those who have the benefit of informal relationships, friendships, access to information and organizational astuteness, tend to thrive in highly political environments. Those who don't are left to filter the moves and turns through heavy reliance on their own personal filters. The reality of organizational politics combined with the nuances or race and gender, add layers of complexity to the black female experience. Individuals and organizations that are serious about moving beyond the status quo, must take action to break though these barriers to business and career advancement.

What Can Organizations and Individuals Do to Support Career Advancement?

The following excerpts came from some of our NMCs.

Dr. Beverly Edgehill: Sometimes CEOs have to make the call. A lot of organizations have gotten people the tools through The Partnership Inc., the ELC, and other sources. The system has not course-corrected. There is a lot of work to be done to change the systematic practices to support career advancement. In the meantime, women must learn to be "tempered radicals" (Meyerson 2003). Stay in the game, and celebrate the progress even though it may not be a lot.

J. Keith Motley, Ph.D.: Networking and having mentors are very important aspects of any strategy to break or go beyond the ceilings. When we achieve a degree of success, we must seek to replicate it in others (through mentoring) so that others can be in a position to build on what we have accomplished. In this way, we acknowledge the iterative nature of our work in this life. We build on the foundations others built. Others should build upon ours.

Elvoid Mayers: Businesses must make a commitment to ensure representation of people of color and professionals need to assert themselves in order to get what they need. You have to advocate for yourself. You must be willing to listen to what is said and what is not said. Your mentor should be someone you really trust. You need good relationships with people of all races. Often times the people who can influence your career are of a different race. You have to work within the framework that you have been given. It is important to build cross-cultural relationships.

Jackie Glenn: There is a glass ceiling. We need to be persistent and must keep pushing. We need to be vigilant about preparing ourselves and other women. Organizations must go beyond making an effort and put resources into the development of women. We need to keep the pressure on. While mentoring relationships are important, they do not have to be formal. I've learned a lot from people whom I admire and observe. It is very important to have sponsorship because it is often the catalyst for career and business advancement.

Martha R.A. Fields: You should have a mentor and be a mentor. Network with a diverse group of people. You will gain another perspective through these relationships. You need to put the world into your networking circle. Network with people in this country and also include others from different parts of the world. Keep up with your network as you move through your various cycles. Over time, people may develop into roles where they may be able to help you or vice versa.

Visael "Bobby" Rodriguez: Gender influences networking. When people talk about the "old boys club," that's a network. When male co-workers have beer night or play golf together, that's a network. Men have a different way of communicating. Men tend to do a lot of their networking around sports, even though they may not call these activities networking.

There is a glass ceiling, even though there are many knowledgeable, talented women who are capable of leading organizations. In order to address this issue, the culture of the organization must change. There tends to be a double standard for women. When a woman is strong, she is often viewed as too strong or too forceful. When a man exhibits the same behaviors, he is often viewed as a strong, decisive leader. The way to change this is to have candid conversations. We need equality in the work environment. Employee resource groups are a place to start. Women also need to shed light on these issues by being mentors and teachers in helping to change the culture.

Patricia Washington: Management teams, starting with the CEO, need to make a public statement that expresses and supports diversity in the broadest sense. Senior leadership needs to be comfortable speaking openly about diversity and inclusion. Furthermore, they need to have a plan and to hold the entire leadership team accountable—not just the diversity officer. Diversity should be a part of the company's strategic plan that is monitored and reported upon at the board level.

For individuals, hone and master your leadership skills—relationship building, presence, negotiation/conflict management, and effectively dealing with people.

Paul Guzzi: The data speaks for itself. There is a glass ceiling, particularly when you look at women in the ranks of C-level positions. Organizations need to prioritize looking for talent and development of talent among women. More focus is needed on the issue. Organizations such as The Boston Club and The Partnership Inc. are helping to bring focus to this important issue.

Individuals should continue to develop formal and informal networks. Authenticity and confidence in who you are <u>and</u> what you have to give are essential. Don't give up! Persist in fulfilling your career and business aspirations.

Carolyn Golden-Hebsgaard: Sometimes you can see through it, and you know the game; other times you can't. It is a concrete ceiling when you can't see what's above you. The ceiling is definitely there, but it cannot be used as a crutch.

Organizations can work on creating an inclusive environment. Policies alone won't do it. You can lay down all kinds of policies. Those things can help, but you need supportive actions from leaders. There is a perception that it is more work to hire someone who is different, but many times leaders don't want to do the work to create an inclusive environment. Those who are willing to do the work should be rewarded and supported.

A few things that women must do:

- **Recognize that there is a different mindset.** It's not just about competence and skill-set. It is also important to observe the behavior of successful women and practice those behaviors. Why are they able to have conversations at a different level? How are they interacting?

- **Observe the culture.** What kind of behaviors are acceptable and propel you forward? Who in the organization is a rainmaker? What are her behaviors? Women can be a lot more observant; look at success factors early on, and adopt some of the behaviors.

Linda Watters: Performance trumps everything. Identify opportunities to tout your achievements and value to the organization at the highest levels. It's a continuous process. Women should seek out strategic initiatives within their organizations and volunteer to work on projects to distinguish themselves from others. Identify a sponsor, and ask them to recommend you for highly visible projects. Once you have performed well, use it as an opportunity to network with senior executives by inviting them to lunch or by scheduling an early morning coffee in their office. The glass ceiling will only shatter if economic pressure is exerted by purchasing goods and services only from those companies who expressly demonstrate and acknowledge the worth of women in the suite and boardroom.

Stacy Blake-Beard, Ph.D.: Research shows that women and people of color tend to have bifurcated networks—one network for support and another for advancement. That's a lot of work. We tend to put our heads down and do the work and keep the relationships separate. We need to look up and think about where we're going and not just focus on the work.

Because we are often one of few, we don't necessarily want to call attention to ourselves because of how it might be misinterpreted. Too often we don't ask for help. The fact is that everyone needs help, but there could be a different cost for us. We could be seen as incapable by asking for help, while others taking the same actions may be viewed as resourceful. It's a double bind for women in general. For women of color there are additional layers and nuances.

Organizations must pay attention to the development of their most important resource—their diverse human talent. It's a critical task facing organizational leaders.

Stay In the Game

NMC leaders gave great advice. Unless acted upon, the observations and insights shared within these pages will become a distant memory. Take a few minutes to think about your role and your sphere of influence. Clearly there is still a lot of work to be done. You have a choice to make. You can opt out or you can stay in the game. My hope is that more people will do the latter and create the critical mass that is necessary to drive meaningful change.

> All the world's a stage,
> And all the men and women merely players.
> They have their exits and their entrances;
> And one man in his time plays many parts...
> —William Shakespeare, "As You Like It"

If It's Going to Be, It's Up to Me

It is time to claim your own power and leverage collective networks—social and business contacts—to leap forward. Everyone must take personal responsibility for bringing about the sea change that will be the tide to lift all boats. It's time to organize and mobilize on an important mantra: "If it's going to be, it's up to me." That doesn't mean that you go it alone, it simply means that you own the portion of the solution and accountability for the actions within your control.

Take Action

Talk the walk and walk the talk. You can bring attention to the issues through conversations and cross-cultural relationships. It is also important to share resources within your sphere of influence—organizations and people who can help to advance the dialogue.

There are lots of well-positioned partners in the struggle for advancement and economic empowerment—white colleagues and business partners as well. Start with your inner circle and your power source, whether that is your church sisters and brothers, community center, family business, or professional organization. Take the pledge today to use your network to affect positive change. For those who are looking for organizations that are serious about facilitating dialogues and programmatically addressing the issues raised in this book, see the "Resources for Organizations and Individuals" in the Appendix.

CHAPTER 10

An Open Letter to my Sisters

CHAPTER 10

An Open Letter to My Sisters

Our deepest fear is not that we are inadequate. Our deepest fear is that we are powerful beyond measure. It is our light, not our darkness, that most frightens us. We ask ourselves, who am I to be brilliant, gorgeous, talented, and fabulous? Actually, who are you not to be? You are a child of God. Your playing small doesn't serve the world. There's nothing enlightened about shrinking so that other people won't feel insecure around you. We are all meant to shine, as children do. We are born to make manifest the glory of God that is within us. It's not just in some of us; it's in everyone. And as we let our own light shine, we unconsciously give other people permission to do the same. As we are liberated from our own fear, our presence automatically liberates others.

—Marianne Williamson

Dear Sisters:

I have vivid memories of my mom's struggle to make ends meet. She was a strong, proud woman who believed in self-reliance, had strong faith in God, and wanted the absolute best for her three daughters. Her belief system clashed sharply with her economic realities, which seemed dire at times. As a single mom for most of her life, my mother was very reluctant to ask for help (a common characteristic among strong black women). I recall being sent to the grocery store during off-peak hours to purchase groceries with food stamps. As the oldest child, my mom would explain that this situation and dependency on welfare was only temporary.

I don't recall how long we were on public assistance; however, I do know how frustrated she was and how reluctant she was to accept help. She used her experiences to school me about the importance of education.

Her vision was to secure the future of her children. She made her objectives abundantly clear and went on to work multiple jobs before landing steady work as a waitress at MIT's Faculty Club. She saw this as an opportunity to learn from others and gain access to resources that were aligned with her vision.

Not only did she articulate her vision, she set goals for me and my sisters. These goals were nonnegotiable. She drove home the message about the importance of education and used herself as an example of what not to do. Her formal schooling ended during elementary school. Her support for me and my sisters came in the form of doing laundry, cooking, cleaning, and freeing up time for us to pursue our studies, part-time work, and extracurricular activities. Her sacrifices ensured maximum focus on the pursuit of the ideals she had for us. She also prayed a lot and articulated her vision: "to see all of her children get as much education as they possibly can."

My mom was a master networker. She did not let her contact with professors and MIT faculty go for naught. She followed the principles of giving, whether it was extra attention at a special luncheon, going beyond expectations on her shift, or helping a fellow waiter. She was beloved and respected for her work. Over the years, she developed a rapport with some of the professors including department heads.

Friendships evolved, and our entire family would be invited to some of the nifty events. She always made sure that we were all dressed to the nines. She understood and exemplified the principles of personal branding: "People judge you by how you carry yourself. Dress properly, and hold your head up high." Great advice.

Success would mean breaking the cycle of poverty, helping her children obtain the degrees that she did not have the opportunity to pursue. We would bring honor to the family name by staying out of trouble and getting good jobs.

My mom's plan was not a formal one, but the principles were similar. She was a strategic networker, although she would not use those words. Through her network, she created access for her children. I now know that my summer internship at Draper Labs at MIT was not by happenstance.

Growing up in poverty both in Barbados and in the United States significantly shaped the person I have become. It is why I am passionate about my work on the board of ABCD. I am committed to fighting poverty and creating pathways to self-sufficiency and education. It is also why I mentor others.

I absolutely have no regrets and believe that the passion and drive that I have today is a direct result of my values, hard work, and help from a lot of people—particularly, my mom.

The fact that you have read this entire book tells me that you are someone who is highly motivated. I hope that you will take the necessary action to drive in the direction of your dreams. In so doing, strive to maintain balance in whatever form that takes for you. Your physical, emotional, and spiritual health are foundational pillars that should never be compromised, so in pursuing your dreams, make the necessary trade-offs to keep these elements intact.

Regardless of your personal circumstance, you have the power within you to affect positive change. When challenges come—not if, because you can count on them—keep hope alive! My prayer for you is that you will embrace and act upon the principles discussed in this book and use the power that is within you to make your dreams a reality.

God Bless,

Juliette C. Mayers

Appendix

Resources for
Organizations and Individuals

This listing is by no means comprehensive. It is reflective of organizations with which I have firsthand experience or knowledge. Summary descriptions from the source websites are included below for your convenience. I encourage you to draw upon your network and trusted advisors to identify the resources that might work best for you and your organization.

Black Enterprise magazine (www.blackenterprise.com)

For many years, *Black Enterprise* magazine has strived to be a catalyst for change and empowerment of black business and black career advancement. In addition to the magazine, Black Enterprise provides access to a wealth of information for small businesses and hosts an annual "Women of Power Summit."

Catalyst (www.catalyst.org)

Founded in 1962, Catalyst is the leading nonprofit membership organization expanding opportunities for women and business. With offices in the U.S. and Canada, Catalysts' work is rooted in research. The organization studies women and men across levels, functions, and geographies to learn about women's experiences in business, barriers to their career advancement, and individual and organizational strategies leading to success. Catalysts' reports are often cited in international media and reveal the challenges and opportunities for organizations and women at work globally. The organization has an extensive compendium of diversity and inclusion practices that provides models for change.

Colette Phillips Communications (www.cpcglobal.com; www.getkonnected.com)

Colette Phillips is CEO of Colette Phillips Communications, the first black-owned public relations firm, and has been at the forefront of bringing people together. Three years ago Colette accelerated her focus on bringing multicultural people together and started Get Konnected, Boston's largest multicultural networking event.

Diversity Woman (http://diversitywoman.com)

Diversity Woman magazine provides business-focused editorial content designed for women business leaders, executives, and entrepreneurs of diverse backgrounds, who have unique interests and concerns. Diversity Woman also plays a mentorship role. Both the magazine and web site serve as a forum and membership directory to connect aspiring businesswomen directly with other women in leadership roles. Much more than a magazine—it is an integrated print, event, and online business with a focus on business and leadership development, mentoring, skill enhancement, and empowerment.

Executive Leadership Council (www.elcinfo.com)

The Executive Leadership Council is the preeminent organization that recognizes the strengths, success, contributions, and impact of African American corporate business leaders. ELC's leadership network is guided by a bold and historic vision of inclusion, which is the leadership legacy of African Americans—whether in business, education, or the community. With more than five hundred members (one-third of them women), the Executive

Leadership Council is the nation's premier leadership organization composed of the most senior African American corporate executives in Fortune 500 companies, representing well over 380 major corporations. The Council represents senior executives in positions one to three levels from the chief executive officers of Fortune 500 companies, CEOs themselves, and other entrepreneurs.

Fields Associates Inc. (www.TheCorporateCupid.com)

Since 1994, Fields Associates has provided expert consulting, educational programs, and inspirational speeches. The company delivers expert solutions to everyday problems and challenges, conferences, provides phenomenal keynote addresses, and consults on key leadership challenges including diversity and inclusion. An internationally renowned speaker and bestselling author, Martha is committed to helping people and organizations reach their fullest potential.

Frasernet (www.frasernet.com)

This website is a wealth of resources. It is run by George Fraser, author of *Success Runs in Our Race* and *Race for Success: The Ten Best Business Opportunities for Blacks in America.* Among many other accomplishments, Mr. Fraser is the creator and publisher of the award-winning *Success Guide Worldwide: The Networking Guide to Black Resources.* He is also the creator of the annual Power Networking Conference, one of black America's largest conferences.

The Boston Club (www.thebostonclub.org)

Founded in 1976, The Boston Club is a community of women executives and professionals that promotes the advancement of women to significant and visible leadership roles. The Boston Club's mission is to impel the advancement of women to top leadership positions across all sectors of the economic landscape.

The Commonwealth Compact (www.commonwealthcompact. umb.edu)

Launched in May 2008, the mission of the Commonwealth Compact is to establish Massachusetts as a uniquely inclusive, honest and supportive community of -- and for -- diverse people. To acknowledge our mixed history in this effort, and to face squarely the challenges that still need to be overcome, understanding that the rich promise of the region's growing diversity must be tapped fully if Boston and Massachusetts are to achieve their economic, civic and social potential.

The organization is committed to making Boston a welcoming, diverse place to live and work for all people.

League of Black Women (www.leagueofblackwomen.org)

League of Black Women (LBW) provides access to strategic support for developing and sustaining leadership values and joyful living for black women. The goal is to ensure that members emerge within their families, communities, workplaces, and various constituencies as exceptional leaders who contribute distinctive, substantial, and lasting improvements to the decisions that shape our world. LBW was established to provide successful, strategic, and sustainable leadership experiences for black women through educational research, promotion of joyful living and improvement of the leadership class of black women.

The Partnership, Inc. (www.thepartnershipinc.org)

The Partnership is leading a new conversation about diversity. It's a conversation that is less about numbers and more about advancement, one that crosses racial, ethnic, and cultural lines. It's a conversation that focuses on solutions rather than problems. The focus is on creating new opportunities for multicultural professionals of color. The Partnership built a new leadership model and launched the first senior executive program that looks at global leadership through a multicultural lens. The Partnership's New

Conversation 2.0 takes its efforts *inside* organizations and works with managers to engage their multicultural employees. The organization supports senior leaders in taking executive action that ensures organization-wide accountability and progress. Everyone has a role in New Conversation 2.0: professionals of color, managers, and senior executives.

The YWCA (www.ywca.org)
The YWCA is the oldest and largest multicultural women's organization in the world. Across the globe, the YWCA has more than 25 million members in 106 countries, including 2.6 million members and participants in 300 local associations in the United States. More important than the numbers is their mission to eliminate racism and empower women. The organization provides safe places for women and girls, builds strong women leaders, and advocates for women's rights and civil rights in Congress.

Glossary of Unique Terms

D-Suite: Roles related to diversity, not an actual classification.

Fro: Abbreviation for afro

H-Suite: Human services role, not an actual classification.

High Value Contact (HVC): Second highest of three strategic networking tiers.

Inner Circle Contacts (ICC): Highest level strategic networking tier.

Moderate Value Contact (MVC): Third tier of the three strategic networking classifications.

Networking Master Class: (NMC): Leaders who have mastered the art networking; it is an integral part of how they operate.

NMC: An abbreviation for Networking Master Class.

Soror(s): An abbreviation for sorority, an organization of women joined together by common interests.

STEM: An acronym for Science Technology Engineering and Math.

W.I.I.F.H.: An abbreviation for What's In It For Her

Bibliography

Bell, Ella L. J. Edmondson, and Stella M. Nkomo. *Our Separate Ways: Black and White Women and the Struggle for Professional Identity*. Boston: Harvard Business School, 2001. Print.

Beaudine, Bob, and Tom Dooley. *The Power of Who: You Already Know Everyone You Need to Know*. New York: Center Street, 2009. Print.

Catalyst, *Advancing African-American Women in the Workplace: What Managers Need to Know* New York: Catalyst Inc. Feb. 2004. Print.

Catalyst, *Connections that Count: The Informal Networks of Women of Color in the United States* Catalyst Inc. May 2006. Print.

Canfield, Jack, Mark Victor Hansen, and Les Hewitt. *The Power of Focus*. Florida: HCI, 2000. Print.

Cobbs, Price M., and Judith L. Turnock. *Cracking the Corporate Code: the Revealing Success Stories of 32 African-American Executives*. New York: American Management Association, 2003. Print.

Feinberg, Jody. "Norwell Mother and Executive Dreams Big and Helps Others Reach Their Goals." *Patriot Ledger* 2 Sept. 2008. Print.

Fields, Martha R.A. *Love Your Work By Loving Your Life*. Cambridge, Massachusetts: Marmerv, 2004. Print.

Fraser, George C. *Success Runs in Our Race: the Complete Guide to Effective Networking in the Black Community*. New York: Amistad, 2004. Print.

Harris, Carla A. *Expect to Win: Proven Strategies for Success from a Wall Street Vet*. New York: Hudson Street, 2009. Print.

Heard, Marian Langston. *The Complete Leader: Your Path to the Top: Tried and True Principles, Good Habits, and Advice to Help You Lead*. Natick, Massachusetts: Heard Enterprises, 2004. Print.

Jordan, Vernon E., and Annette Gordon-Reed. *Vernon Can Read! A Memoir*. New York: Basic Civitas, 2003. Print.

Latifah, Queen, and Karen Hunter. *Ladies First: Revelations of a Strong Woman*. New York: William Morrow, 1999. Print.

Meyerson, Debra E. *Tempered Radicals: How Everyday Leaders Inspire Change at Work*. Boston: Harvard Business School Press, June 2003. Print.

Meyerson, Debra and Joanne Martin. *Women and Power: Conformity, Resistance and Disorganized Coaction*. (Power and Influence by Roderick M. Kramer and Margaret A. Neale) Sage Publications Inc. Thousand Oaks, CA. 1998. Print

Misner, Ivan R., David G. Alexander, and Brian Hilliard. *Networking like a Pro: Turning Contacts into Connections*. [Irvine, Calif.]: Entrepreneur, 2009. Print.

Rutledge, Patricia Anne. *Sams Teach Yourself LinkedIn*, Sams/Pearson, 2011. Print.

Schawbel, Dan. *Me 2.0: 4 Steps to Building Your Future*. New York: Kaplan Pub., 2010. Print.

Scott, David Meerman. *The New Rules of Marketing and PR: How to Use Social Media, Blogs, News Releases, Online Video, & Viral Marketing to Reach Buyers Directly*. Hoboken, NJ: John Wiley & Sons, 2010. Print.

Shih, Clara Chung-wai. *The Facebook Era: Tapping Online Social Networks to Market, Sell, and Innovate*. Upper Saddle River, NJ: Prentice Hall, 2011. Print.

Sue, Derald Wing. *Microaggressions in Everyday Life: Race, Gender, and Sexual Orientation*. Hoboken, NJ: Wiley, 2010. Print.

Thomas, David A., and John J. Gabarro. *Breaking Through: The Making of Minority Executives in Corporate America*. Boston: HBS, 1999. HBS Press. Web.

"Women of Color in Corporate Management: Opportunities and Barriers." *Catalyst* (1999).

WOW Facts. Diversity Best Practices. *Diversity Best Practices*| Diversity Best Practices, 2011. Web. 08 July 2011. <http://www.diversitybestpractices.com/news-publications/wow-facts>.

THE END

ABOUT THE AUTHOR

Juliette C. Mayers

Juliette Mayers is a marketing executive at Blue Cross Blue Shield of Massachusetts. She is an award-winning executive, business strategist, and a passionate community advocate.

In 2010, Massachusetts Governor Deval Patrick appointed her to the Massachusetts Workforce Investment Board, a state-wide policy making board that advises the governor on workforce investment. Among her many civic and leadership positions, Juliette is Emeritus Board President of Action for Boston Community Development (ABCD), a $150 million anti-poverty organization and the largest community action agency in the country.

A networking guru, Mayers is an author, speaker and mentor to a diverse group of women and a *few good men*. She is an alumna of Simmons Graduate School of Management where she earned her MBA. A native of Barbados West Indies, Juliette is married to attorney Darryl Mayers and resides in Norwell, MA with her husband and two teen-aged daughters, D'Anna and Danielle.

www.juliettemayers.com

Index